CHRISTOPHER DURANG was born in 1950. While attending Harvard, he spent vast numbers of his waking hours watching old movies, forming the cinematic reservoir of images and characters from which *A History of the American Film* was created. He earned a M.F.A. degree from the Yale School of Drama, where he won the CBS Playwriting Prize for *The Idiots Karamazov*, coauthored by Albert Innaurato. In 1976 he was accepted at the Eugene O'Neill National Playwrights Conference with *A History of the American Film*; subsequently, the play was given an unprecedented tri-city premiere in Hartford, Los Angeles, and Washington, D.C. He was the recipient of a CBS Foundation Fellowship in Playwriting and a Rockefeller Foundation grant. His other plays include *The Vietnamization of New Jersey, When Dinah Shore Ruled the World* (coauthored by Wendy Wasserstein), *The Nature and Purpose of the Universe, Titanic,* and *Das Lusitania Songspiel* (coauthored by Sigourney Weaver).

A HISTORY OF THE
AMERICAN FILM

by CHRISTOPHER DURANG

A BARD BOOK/PUBLISHED BY AVON BOOKS

Based on the poster design by Jon Anthony Rodriguez.

AVON BOOKS
A division of
The Hearst Corporation
959 Eighth Avenue
New York, New York 10019

First Bard Printing, June, 1978

BARD TRADEMARK REG. U.S. PAT. OFF. AND IN
OTHER COUNTRIES, MARCA REGISTRADA, HECHO EN
U.S.A.

Printed in the U.S.A.

A History of the American Film was given its first New York production at the ANTA Theatre on March 30, 1978. It was produced by Richard S. Bright and Judith Gordon. Music by Mel Marvin. Directed by David Chambers. Scenery designed by Tony Straiges. Costumes by Marjorie Slaiman. Lighting by William Mintzer. Musical staging by Graciela Daniele. Sound design by Lou Shapiro. Musical direction by Clay Fullum. Orchestrations by Robert M. Freeman. The cast was as follows:

Loretta	April Shawhan
Jimmy	Gary Bayer
Bette	Swoosie Kurtz
Hank	Brent Spiner
Eve	Joan Pape
Clara Mortimer	Mary Catherine Wright
Michael O'Reilly	Walter Bobbie
Piano Man, Viola, Ito, etc.	Ben Halley, Jr.
Blessed Mother, Ma Joad, etc.	Maureen Anderson
Allison, Ma O'Reilly, etc.	Kate McGregor-Stewart
Victor Henreid, Edward, etc.	Bryan Clark
Mickey, Newsboy	Jeff Brooks
Abdhul, Pa Joad, Harkness, etc.	David Cromwell
David	David Garrison
Eric	Eric Weitz

Prior to the New York production, the play was first performed at the Eugene O'Neill Memorial Theatre Foundation in Waterford, Connecticut; and, as a joint premiere, in three separate productions at the Hartford Stage Co., the Mark Taper Forum in Los Angeles, and the Arena Stage in Washington, D.C.

LIST OF CHARACTERS

The Stars:
Loretta   Jimmy   Bette   Eve   Hank

The Contract Players:
(a group of ten actors who play the following
roles with much doubling)

The Mother	Ma Joad
Policeman	Pa Joad
God	Grandma Joad
Jesus	Prison Warden
Blessed Mother	Christmas Carolers
Orphanage Lady	Santa Claus
Minstrel Singer	Indian
Ticket Man	Mickey
Newsboy	Fritz von Leffing
Ma O'Reilly	Salad Girls
Michael O'Reilly	Chef
Gangsters, B-Girls	Dolores del Reego
Ferruchi	Makeup Artist
Henchmen	Harkness, a Butler
Judge	Piano Man
Lawyer	Ito
Reporters	Opera Peasants
Nurse	Movie Patron
David	Victor Henreid
Eric	Three Singing Sisters
Viola, a Maid	Robot
Clara Mortimer	Alcoholics
Edward Mortimer	Prison Matron
Allison Mortimer	Stuart
Abdhul	Theater Manager

THE SETTING

In the productions designed by Tony Straiges
(Arena Stage and the New York production),
the play is set in a large, nonrealistic movie
palace. This movie palace has an upstage balcony, behind which is a movie projection booth
(which later explodes); it has two small side
balconies, right and left, which represent at
various times an opera box, Hoboken, and heaven. On the stage floor are ten or fifteen movie
theater seats (on rollers, for fast movement),
which, spaced irregularly and with members of
the cast seated in them, suggest a movie audience. For the non-movie house sections of the
play, these seats either are removed or else stand
in for regular furniture (as in the gangster and
screwball comedy sections).

In the scenes that take place specifically in
the movie house, the actors stare out ahead of
them, as if the film they are watching were just
over the live audience's heads.

Act I is performed in black and white—that
is, the costumes and props are black, gray, and
white only. (Face, hair, lip color should be left

normal.) The movie palace set at Arena was painted gray and silver so as not to contradict this.

The play turns to color at the end of Act I, as specified in the script.

The play at Arena Stage began with most of the cast seated in the movie house seats, staring out, waiting for the movie to begin. A screen (upstage, behind the actors' heads—the actors pretended to see it in front of them) was lowered, having popular songs of the twenties projected on it. The actors and audience both had a pre-show, follow-the-bouncing-ball sing-along. At the finish of this, the lights dimmed, piano silent-movie music was played, and the play proper began.

ACT ONE

Scene 1

A motherly woman in old-fashioned clothes sits rocking a large cradle in one area of the stage.
Title: *"Out of the cradle, endlessly rocking . . ."*
Lights dim on this image.
Lights up again on same woman (the MOTHER*).*
The MOTHER, *after a moment of rocking, frowns, takes the baby from the cradle, walks across the stage, and places it on a doorstep. (Another area of the stage, which lights up as she gets there. Lights remain on the cradle area also.) The* MOTHER *hesitates, then resolutely leaves the child there, returning to her chair by the cradle.*
Title: *"The Selfish Mother gets into the cradle herself."*
The MOTHER *does this. Lights remain on her as she rocks.*
A POLICEMAN *comes by "doorstep" and sees the child, does large take, and speaks soundlessly.*
Title: *"A foundling!"*
He picks the child up, exits. Lights fade on whole stage.
Complete dark.
Title: *"Time passes."*

Lights up on the MOTHER, *still in the cradle. She coughs silently, very ill. She prays.*

Title: *"Near death, the Mother prays to God to forgive her for deserting her child."*

Lights up in heaven. GOD *(with white beard),* JESUS *(with sacred heart on his white robe), and the* BLESSED MOTHER *talk silently together, perhaps pointing down toward the* MOTHER.

Title: *"God refuses to forgive her."*

The MOTHER *is crushed by their refusal, weeps.*

Title: *"The Mother dies."*

The MOTHER *dies. Lights fade off her area.*

Up in heaven. The BLESSED MOTHER *talks with* GOD *and* JESUS, *makes motion of rocking baby in her arms.*

Title: *"But what has happened to the baby? Can we help it?"*

GOD *looks stern and speaks to the* BLESSED MOTHER.

Title: *"It is not up to Us to help those on earth. We can only watch."*

The Three look down and watch. As the lights dim down on them, the lights dim up on the following:

Enter LORETTA, *a young, tall ingenue, very lovely in a white dress. She gives the audience the look of a startled fawn.*

Title: *"The baby grows up to be a lovely girl in the orphanage."*

Enter the ORPHANAGE LADY, *who hands* LORETTA *a small suitcase and points away.*

Title: *"Loretta is told she is too tall to remain*

in the Home but must make her own way now."
LORETTA *hesitates, worries, takes the suitcase. The* ORPHANAGE LADY *hands her a coin.*
Title: *"Here is a nickel. Spend it wisely."*
LORETTA *smiles, takes it, and starts to walk slowly away.* ORPHANAGE LADY *waves and exits (walking backwards).*
LORETTA *walks about the stage (from pool of light to pool of light?).*
A MINSTREL SINGER *in black face is lit, singing silently.* LORETTA *looks interested. A* TICKET MAN *appears and bars her from coming too close, unless she pays him the nickel.*
Title: *"Loretta reluctantly pays the nickel."*
Loretta sits down to watch the MINSTREL SINGER. *He finishes what he's been singing and is ready to sing a new one.*
A musical introduction to the MINSTREL SINGER's *song is heard over the sound system. The* MINSTREL SINGER's *voice is on the "sound track" and the actor playing the* MINSTREL SINGER *mimes the song along, noticeably out of synch. At the very end of the song the actor's real voice can be heard as the sound track voice fades out. Thus the recorded voice fades into the live voice.*

MINSTREL. [*Miming sound track*]
The sun shines south,
The sun shines north,
And Lazarus, he's a-comin' forth,
But I'm alone with my song,

11

And I guess I better move along,
I'm goin' back to my dear old Alabammy,
And sleep in the bosom of my Mammy. . . .
    Mammy, cradle me and hold me,
    Mammy, the Massuh's gone and sold me,
    Mammy, I'm sick a pickin' cotton,
    Mammy, I know you ain't forgotten,
And so I'm comin' back,
To that old shack,
And see my MA–A–AMY!

[LORETTA *cries*.]
Title: *"Loretta's heart is wrenched apart by the word 'Mammy.'"*
[*Lights fade to an "iris" spot on* LORETTA.]

BLACKOUT

Scene 2

Overamplified sounds of a city park (cars in the distance played on a scratchy tape). A very prominent microphone is lowered. LORETTA *looks about, at a loss where to go. Enter a* POLICEMAN *(perhaps same one as before).*

POLICEMAN. Whaddya doin' there, young lady?

LORETTA. Nothing, Officer.

POLICEMAN. Well, a nice girl oughtn't to be

about on the streets at this hour. Shanty Town's not a safe place for a nice girl.

LORETTA. Yes, Officer.

POLICEMAN. [*Kindly*] Run along home now, miss. [*She nods. He exits.*]

LORETTA. Yes, Officer. Oh, look, a kitty. Hello, kitty, hello. Oh, it's someone's hair. Oh. [*A bit alarmed*] Officer! [*He's gone.*] Oh dear, oh dear. Nowhere to go, just like that little kitty. That's right, it wasn't a kitty. [*Shudders.*] Maybe if I sleep, things will be better. [*Sits on park bench to sleep.*]
[*Enter a* NEWSBOY *with a cap on his head, holding newspapers.*]

NEWSBOY. Extra, extra, read all about it. Unemployment Reaches New Low Point. Hoover Appoints Commission to Study. Extra, extra, read all about it. St. Valentine's Massacre Marks Peak of Gangster Wars. Extra, extra, Garbo Talks in Metro Movie. Says, "Gif Me a Whiskey, Ginger Ale on the Side, and Don't Be Stingy, Baby." Extra, extra. Actor John Gilbert Unable to Make Transition to Talkies. Hoover Appoints Commission to Study. [*To* LORETTA.] Paper, miss?

LORETTA. Oh . . . I don't have any money.

NEWSBOY. Here ya go, miss. [*Gives her one.*]

LORETTA. Oh, thank you.

NEWSBOY. [*Going off.*] Extra, extra, read all about it. Unemployment Reaches New Low Point. Hoover Appoints Commission to Study. . . .

LORETTA. [*Reading to herself at same time* NEWSBOY *says it.*] Unemployment reaches new low point. Hoover appoints commission to study. [*Yawns.*]

NEWSBOY. [*From offstage*] Extra, extra, read all about it. [*His voice gets sleepy, as if heard through* LORETTA'*s sleepiness.*] St. Valentine's Massacre Marks Peak of Gangsterrr Warssss. . . . Extra, extra. . . .
[LORETTA *falls asleep. Lights dim.*]

BLACKOUT

Scene 3

SOUND: *of birds chirping. Lights up, it's morning.* LORETTA *is asleep on the park bench. Next to her is* JIMMY, *a young and energetic tough. He is also asleep, with his hat over his face. This holds for a moment.* JIMMY *mumbles in his sleep a bit, then suddenly jerks awake and fires his gun.* LORETTA *screams awake.*

JIMMY. Take that, you dirty copper! [*Looks*

about, sees he's been dreaming. LORETTA *looks at him aghast.*] Whatsa matter, I wake you? [*Pause.*] Say, you're a pretty scrawny-looking lamb chop, ain't ya?

LORETTA. [*Feeling very faint from hunger.*] I feel . . .

JIMMY. I bet you could *use* a good lamb chop, couldn't ya? Ya hungry?

LORETTA. [*Mumbles.*] I . . . need . . .

JIMMY. Hey, Sadie, speak up. [*He pokes her; she whimpers; he listens closely to her.*]

LORETTA. [*Softly*] Get me . . .

JIMMY. Yeah, get me. Get me what?

LORETTA. . . . Get me . . . to . . .

JIMMY. Get me two. Two what? Two lamb chops? Two chickens? Two steaks?

LORETTA. . . . Get me . . . to . . . the hospital. . . .

JIMMY. Hospital? Whatsa matter?

LORETTA. Can you help me?

JIMMY. I'm American, ain't I?
[JIMMY *helps* LORETTA *off the bench. Lights fade*

*on this area, fade up on another area, represent-
ing* JIMMY's *shack in Shanty Town. Music plays
on the sound track while he moves her. They
arrive at the shack.*]

JIMMY. Well, here we are. It ain't much, but I
call it home. [*Sits her down.*] Hey, sourpuss,
howd'ya like it?

LORETTA. It's very nice.

JIMMY. Call me Jimmy, why don'tcha?

LORETTA. Okay, Jimmy.

JIMMY. That's the ticket. We gotta get you
well.

LORETTA. Thank you. [*Begins to faint.*]

JIMMY. Hey, now, none of that. [*Sits her up.*]
Where ya from, sourpuss?

LORETTA. I'm from an orphanage.

JIMMY. Oh yeah?

LORETTA. Are you an orphan too?

JIMMY. Nah, I got a ma, but I spent most of my
time in a reform school.

LORETTA. You did?

JIMMY. What's wrong wid that?

LORETTA. [*Scared*] Nothing. Why were you put in reform school?

JIMMY. For robbin' the poor box at St. Raphael's and settin' Fadder MacNeil on fire.

LORETTA. Jimmy, you didn't.

JIMMY. Sure I did. I sang in the choir, too. Fadder MacNeil was a real dodo anyways. I liked seein' him on fire.

LORETTA. Did he die?

JIMMY. Nah. It's hard to kill priests.

LORETTA. But did reform school change you?

JIMMY. Yeah, I'd never try to burn somebody anymore. I'd shoot 'im.
[*There is a sudden clap of thunder and flash of lightning.* LORETTA *screams and inadvertently embraces* JIMMY.]

LORETTA. What was that?

JIMMY. Whaddya t'ink it was?

LORETTA. It sounds like a storm. [*She moves away from him a bit.*]

JIMMY. Whatsa matter? You scared of me?

LORETTA. A little.

JIMMY. Ah, relax, sourpuss. I ain't gonna bite
ya.
[SOUND: *of the rain coming down, steadily, on
the roof. Music introduction of a romantic song
begins.* JIMMY *starts to sing in a soft Bing Crosby
style.*]

[*Sings*]
Hear the pitter patter on the roof,
The raindrops sing a pleasant song,
Pennies fall from heaven up above,
Inside, we're cozy and in love,
The roof may leak but we don't care,
We have a future life to share,
Anyone could tell it at a glance,
We share a SHANTY TOWN ROMANCE.

It's not the Ritz,
It's not the Riviera,
Who wants a villa in Rome,
When you've got a Shanty Town home. . . .

[LORETTA *joins him, singing.*]
Hear the pitter patter on the roof,
The raindrops say that nothing's wrong,
Pennies fall from heaven up above,
Inside, we're sleepy and in love,
Anyone could tell it at a glance,
We share a SHANTY TOWN, a SHANTY
    TOWN, a SHANTY TOWN ROMANCE.

LORETTA. Oh, Jimmy. When you sing to me,

I don't mind being poor at all. And I know whatever happens, everything's going to be all right.

[LORETTA *rests in* JIMMY's *arms.* SOUND TRACK *plays theme of "Shanty Town Romance." As lights dim on them, lights dim up on a large calendar whose daily leaves fall off one at a time, signifying time passing. Lights then dim on the calendar, and the scene's over.*]

BLACKOUT

Scene 4

The shack, some time later. LORETTA *is alone, ironing a shirt on the kitchen table and humming to herself.*

LORETTA. [*Singing to herself without accompaniment*]
It's not the Ritz,
It's not the Riviera,
Who wants a . . .
[*Enter* BETTE, *a tough-looking woman in a print dress.*]

BETTE. Hey, Jimmy, I'm back. . . . [*Sees* LORETTA, *stares.*]

LORETTA. Oh, hello. I'm ironing.

BETTE. Oh?

19

LORETTA. Are you a friend of Jimmy's?

BETTE. Yeah. Who are you?

LORETTA. I'm Loretta. Jimmy's letting me stay here until I'm well.

BETTE. Oh yeah? How ya feelin'?

LORETTA. Well, I still feel a little weak.

BETTE. You look weak. Look, sister, I'll give you five minutes to pack your things and get yourself outa here.

LORETTA. But . . . I'm ironing.

BETTE. I'm very good at ironing. [*Picks up iron.*] How d'ya like your face done, honey—starch or no starch?
[LORETTA *screams. Enter* JIMMY.]

JIMMY. Hey. What's this?

BETTE. Just givin' a couple of pointers on how to do your shirts, Jimmy.

JIMMY. Look, baby, let's get one thing straight —you ain't never done my shirts.

BETTE. But . . .

JIMMY. We're through, Bette.

20

BETTE. But . . .

JIMMY. Cut the small talk. [*To* BETTE] Whatcha hear when you wuz in Chicago?

BETTE. Louie the Hook says you don't guarantee his beer in town and he's gonna put on the squeeze.

LORETTA. But beer is prohibited.
[JIMMY *and* BETTE *stare at her*.]

JIMMY. [*To* BETTE] And Ferruchi's boys?

BETTE. They're standing by Louie. You don't take his beer, your speakeasy don't stay open.

LORETTA. Speakeasy!

BETTE. You should get her a monkey and put her on the stage.

JIMMY. Lay off her, Bette. She don't mean nothin'.

LORETTA. I mean something.

JIMMY. Keep outa this, sourpuss.

BETTE. Sourpuss. That's cute.

JIMMY. Beat it, Bette. I wanna talk to Loretta.

BETTE. [*Hurt*] Okay, Jimmy. [*To* LORETTA]

Good-bye, sourpuss. Hope to see you again real soon—preferably on the obituary page. [*Exits.*]

LORETTA. She took the iron.

JIMMY. Look, bright eyes, I don't want you givin' me no advice about how to run my business, you got me?

LORETTA. But if something isn't legal . . .

JIMMY. I got big plans. You think I wanna live in this dump forever?

LORETTA. But I love it here.

JIMMY. Boy, you're a real fruitcake, you know that?
[SOUND: *of rain falling.* LORETTA *looks up happily.*]

LORETTA. Jimmy, what does happiness feel like?

JIMMY. Whatcha wanna know for?

LORETTA. Because I think I'm happy.
[SOUND: *of rain, louder. Music of "Shanty Town Romance" also. Lights dim.*]

BLACKOUT

Scene 5

The same, some time later, breakfast. LORETTA *and* JIMMY *eating grapefruit.*

LORETTA. Jimmy, can we get married?

JIMMY. What's eatin' you?

LORETTA. Jimmy, I'm going to have a baby, and I want him to have a name.

JIMMY. Why don't you call him nitwit? Jeez, you dames is all alike.

LORETTA. Jimmy, every baby should have a mother *and* fa—

JIMMY. Yeah? You wanna know what I think of that?
[JIMMY *violently pushes his grapefruit in her face.*]

BLACKOUT

Scene 6

A living room. LORETTA *sits on a sofa with Jimmy's mother,* MA O'REILLY. MA *has a large photograph album on her lap.*

MA O'REILLY. And here's a picture of Jimmy

when he was two and a half. And here's a picture of Jimmy when he was three. And here's Jimmy when he was four.
[LORETTA *cries*.]

LORETTA. Oh, Mrs. O'Reilly, I'm so ashamed. I've come to see you because I haven't seen Jimmy in six months and I'm going to have his baby.

MA O'REILLY. And here's Jimmy when he was five.

LORETTA. Mrs. O'Reilly, didn't you hear me?

MA O'REILLY. Yes, I heard you, but I was thinking. Maybe you should talk to my other son. Michael!
[*Enter* MICHAEL, *Jimmy's policeman brother, upstanding and serious-looking.*]

MICHAEL. Yes, Ma.

MA O'REILLY. Oh, Michael . . . [*She cries; so does* LORETTA.]

MICHAEL. It's Jimmy again, isn't it? Why do you cry, Ma? You know he's no good.

MA O'REILLY. Michael was always the good boy, and he became a policeman, but Jimmy had a harder time of it. He was too short for the police force.

MICHAEL. He's a rat, Ma.

MA O'REILLY. It's the environment that made him be bad. If a boy grows up on a city street and he's poor and there are other poor boys playing on the street, why, then he's bound to get confused.

MICHAEL. I didn't get confused.

MA O'REILLY. I know, but you fought in the world war and that made you think straight, but Jimmy didn't have that advantage, and the streets don't teach you what's right and wrong. [To LORETTA] Were you brought up on the street?

LORETTA. No. I was brought up in an orphanage. I have no excuse.

MA O'REILLY. That's an excuse. A lot of orphans become criminals because they have no love.

LORETTA. I wish I had a mother.

MA O'REILLY. I have a daughter, but I always liked Jimmy the best, didn't I, Michael?

MICHAEL. He's a crook and a killer, Ma.

MA O'REILLY. It's not his fault, Michael. It's the society.

MICHAEL. [*To* LORETTA] Come on, miss, we'll
find that rat if we have to look in every
crummy gin joint and speakeasy in the whole
state. [*He takes* LORETTA *out.*]

MA O'REILLY. Tell him I'm making corned
beef for supper, Michael. He always liked
that. [*Gets on her hands and knees and scrubs
the floor with a hard hand brush.*] Poor Jimmy.
[*Scrubs.*]

BLACKOUT

Scene 7

JIMMY's *speakeasy.* JIMMY *sits at a table by himself. Gangsterish men and a few B-girl types are
also about. As scene opens,* BETTE, *in glittering
gown, is in a spotlight, singing.*

BETTE.
They can take away my whiskey,
And my vodka and champagne,
They can take my rubbing alcohol,
And pour it down the drain,
They can take my sloe gin fizz away,
But, baby, then here's what I say,
THEY CAN'T PROHIBIT LOVE!
They can toss my bourbon out the door,
But, baby, like I said before,
THEY CAN'T PROHIBIT LOVE!
We'd make it in the bathtub!

THEY CAN'T PROHIBIT LOVE!
[*Applause.* BETTE *bows, comes over to* JIMMY, *looks concerned.*]

BETTE. Jimmy, you promised you wuz gonna lay low.

JIMMY. I ain't layin' low for Ferruchi or anybody else.

BETTE. Ferruchi and his boys are gunnin' for ya, ya big lug.

JIMMY. Don't ride me, Bette.

BETTE. Oh, go ahead, get killed, see if I care. [*Cries, takes handkerchief from her purse.*]

JIMMY. You're really stuck on me, ain't ya?

BETTE. Oh, go drink your beer.

JIMMY. [*Sees a gun in her purse, holds it up.*] Since when you start carryin' hardware?

BETTE. [*Recklessly unhappy*] It ain't nothin'. It's a cigarette lighter. [*Puts cigarette in her mouth, aims gun at it, shoots it in half; sudden dead silence in the speakeasy.*]

JIMMY. What are you, crazy? [*Speakeasy noise starts up again.*]

BETTE. I love ya, Jimmy.

JIMMY. You coulda shot your nose off.

BETTE. What do I need my nose for? You don't love me.

JIMMY. [*Puts the gun back in her purse.*] You dames is drivin' me crazy.
[*Enter* MICHAEL, *in his police uniform, and* LORETTA. *All noise stops.*]

SOMEONE. It's the cops!

JIMMY. It's Okay. It's my brudder. [MICHAEL *and* LORETTA *come to him.*] Hiya, Mike. How's Ma?

MICHAEL. She prays for ya, Jimmy.

JIMMY. That's nice.

MICHAEL. She doesn't want you to be a gangster, Jimmy.

JIMMY. And I don't want her to be a gangster.

LORETTA. Michael, leave me with Jimmy, please.
[MICHAEL *exits.*]

JIMMY. Hiya, sourpuss. Whatcha drinkin'?

LORETTA. I don't drink, Jimmy.

BETTE. You wanna know why nobody likes you? 'Cause you're so good you're dull.

JIMMY. And what makes you think a B-girl's so interesting? Beat it, Bette.
[BETTE, *extremely stung, gasps, moves away.*]

JIMMY. Whaddya want, Loretta?

LORETTA. I want a proper life. I want every transgression to be punished. I want no conversation to have salacious content. I want never to discuss themes of incest or white slavery. I want to be a married wife and have children and have a bedroom with two beds in it and when you're on the bed you have to always keep one foot on the floor. That's what I want.

JIMMY. Loretta, you're a good kid. But I ain't the marryin' kind. I'm a rat, Loretta. You don't wanna marry a rat.

LORETTA. Yes I do. [*Cries.*]

JIMMY. Here, honk on this. [*Offers her his handkerchief.*]

LORETTA. Thank you, I have my own. [*She opens* BETTE's *purse, thinking it's her own; takes out* BETTE's *gun.*] Oh. This isn't mine. I . . .
[FERRUCHI AND HIS HENCHMEN *burst into the*

room and machine-gun JIMMY *to death. Then they rush out.*]

LORETTA. [*Still holding* BETTE's *gun.*] JIMMY!

BETTE. JIMMY!
[*Enter* MA O'REILLY, *hysterical.*]

MA O'REILLY. JIIIIIIIIMMMMMMMMMMM-
   YYYYYYYYY!
[*Enter* MICHAEL, *stands by the dying* JIMMY *and* MA.]

MICHAEL. [*Looking at* JIMMY.] They all end
   this way, every one of them.

JIMMY. [*Dying.*] Mother of God, is this the end
   of Jimmy O'Reilly? [*Dies.*]
[*A large* THE END *sign, in cut-out letters, is low-ered in front of this tableau.* SOUND: *gangster music soars, crescendoes, finishes as at end of movie. Everyone holds this. Music stops. The* THE END *sign goes up again. The characters—as opposed to the actors—seem a trifle surprised that they have to go on with their lives, as if they had expected to stay frozen behind the* THE END *sign forever.*
After a bit of silence, BETTE *breaks the impasse by breaking into hysterics.*]

BETTE. [*Pointing to* LORETTA, *who still holds*

the gun.] She did it! I saw her! She killed Jimmy!`

LORETTA. That's a lie.

MA O'REILLY. My son, my son!

BETTE. Murderess! Murderess!

MA O'REILLY. I made you corned beef for supper, Jimmy.

BETTE. She did it! She killed Jimmy!

LORETTA. That's a lie.
[MICHAEL *tries to comfort* MA O'REILLY]

MA O'REILLY. [*to* MICHAEL] Take your hands off me! My only son is dead!
[*During the commotion the* JUDGE *enters with gavel.*]

JUDGE. Order in the court, order in the court.
[LORETTA *is in the witness box. On the side are* BETTE, MA O'REILLY, *and* MICHAEL.
Also present, to the side, are three reporters: EVE *(in a woman's business suit and a hat) and two male reporters; all three hold telephones.*]

JUDGE. If there is another such outburst I shall have to clear the courtroom.

MICHAEL. [*To* LORETTA] Did you on the night of November 23 kill James T. O'Reilly?

LORETTA. Please, Michael, I'm going to have a baby.

JUDGE. What did she say?

LAWYER. She said she's going to have a baby. His baby.

JUDGE. Now? [LORETTA *starts to have birth pangs.*] Get a nurse in here.
[*A* NURSE *enters, helps* LORETTA *off. The* REPORTERS *spring into action, each holding his own telephone.*]

EVE.
Jack, it's Eve down at the courtroom, get this down: A hushed courtroom viewed the fourth day of the murder trial of Loretta Moran, a beautiful orphan girl from the wrong side of the tracks, accused of killing her parttime gangster husband. . . .

REPORTER NUMBER 1.
Okay, Louie, tell 'em to hold the front page and get your pencil. It's pandemonium down here as Loretta Moran is in the back room giving birth to a baby. The crowd's goin' wild, shouting and throwin' paper cups and bottles. . . .

REPORTER NUMBER 2.
Hello, Harry? It's Ernie. No. Nothing much new. The dame's gonna have a baby. How are you doin'? Win anything at the horses? . . .

[*The* REPORTERS' *voices trail off, and courtroom noise stops, when all see that the* NURSE *has grimly reentered the room.*]

NURSE. The baby is dead.
[*Pandemonium breaks out.* MA O'REILLY *faints.* MICHAEL *and* BETTE *help her off, with great difficulty* JUDGE *bangs his gavel. Most of the audi-*

ence focus should go to the three REPORTERS, *who are shouting back into their phones.*]

EVE.	REPORTER NUMBER 1.	REPORTER NUMBER 2.
Jack, listen fast: Death in the courtroom. Loretta Moran has a dead lover and now she has a dead baby, too. Minutes after court was called to order. . . .	Hey, Louie, you hear that? Dead as a doornail and closed as a clamshell. Boy, this Moran kid's really got the breaks. As the courtroom erupts. . . .	Hey, Harry? The dame's kid's kicked off. Yeah. Too bad. How's your kid? What? Say, who is this? I wanted Tarryton 9-8760. What number is this?

[*The* REPORTERS' *voices trail off again as* LORETTA *walks slowly back into the courtroom. Lights should dim now, leaving a spot on* LORETTA, *a spot on the* JUDGE, *and an area on the* REPORTERS, *especially* EVE.]

JUDGE. Loretta Moran, you have been found guilty of murder in the first degree, and it is the duty of this court to sentence you. In view of your unfortunate state in life, but mindful of the seriousness of your crime, I sentence you to twenty-five years' hard labor on a chain gang. [*Bangs gavel.* LORETTA *gasps.*]

[*Lights focus on* LORETTA. JUDGE's *voice is heard in an echo-chamber effect.*]

. . . *twenty-five years' hard labor on a chain gang . . . twenty-five years' hard labor on a chain gang. . . .*

[*Lights spot* LORETTA *alone.* EVE *is on the phone again. The two male* REPORTERS *play cards or shoot dice.*]

EVE. Jack? It's Eve again. Get your pencil ready. Orphan Girl Sentenced to Chain Gang.

Loretta Moran. No mother. No father. Nobody to love but a gangster husband and, for a few minutes, a baby. But somehow love wasn't enough. If you want it too bad, love's never enough. But it wasn't just love that finished off Loretta Moran. It was the gangs; it was the system; and it was the world. [*Pause.*] Well, that closes the last chapter on the Loretta Moran case. What? Yeah, I want a chicken on rye with lots of mayo and scratch the pickle. [*Hangs up, exits.*]

[*The spot intensifies on* LORETTA. SOUND: *Prison movie music crescendoes. The* THE END *sign lowers itself in front of* LORETTA's *despairing face. The music finishes. Complete blackout.*]

Scene 8

In the down-right balcony, the lights pick up DAVID *and* ERIC, *who applaud the preceding gangster movie and who have been sitting in the balcony, eating popcorn and watching the imaginary screen, since the beginning of the speakeasy scene. They are young boys, dressed in 1930s Dead End Kid clothes, looking fifteen or seventeen;* DAVID *is the taller, more worldly;* ERIC *is short, younger-looking.*

ERIC. Wasn't that great!

DAVID. Yeah, it was pretty good.

34

ERIC. I like the part when he pushes the grapefruit in her face. [*He imitates* JIMMY'*s motion with the grapefruit.*] I'm gonna do that to *my* girl friend.

DAVID. You don't have a girl friend.

ERIC. Well, when I get one.

DAVID. You're not going to get a girl friend. You're too short.

ERIC. Jimmy is short.

DAVID. Not as short as you.

ERIC. Yes he is.

DAVID. He isn't.

ERIC. Yes he is.

DAVID. No he isn't.

ERIC. He is.

DAVID. He isn't.

ERIC. SHUT UP! [*Pushes popcorn bag in* DAVID'*s face.*] I wanna see the next feature.

Scene 9

DAVID *and* ERIC *look out to screen, and we begin the next feature.*

Cheerful music is heard on the sound track. Lights come up as a phone rings. The lighting in the previous scenes has been Warner Brothers ominous—harsh, with lots of shadows. Now the lighting should be Paramount romantic—very bright, soft.

Enter VIOLA, *a heavy colored maid in a frilly uniform, to answer the phone.*

VIOLA. [*Answering phone, very slurred accent*] Hlo, Misser-en-Misszzes Morimers' reszdence. No, I'm sorry, Misszzes Morimer isn't heah. She out on a scabinger hunt. Scabinger. S–K–E... [*Thinks.*] ...I–B–Z–R–Y, Scabinger. Ahright, thank *you.*

[*Enter a young heiress,* CLARA MORTIMER, *dressed in a shiny negligee.*]

CLARA. Was that for me, Viola?

VIOLA. No, Miz Claha, dat done be for Misszzes Morimer.

CLARA. Oh, why are there never any calls for me, Viola?

VIOLA. I jus' doan' know, Miz Claha. [*Plops down, opens up a box of chocolates, eats them voraciously.*]

CLARA. [*Plopping down in another chair.*] I'm pretty, I'm reasonably intelligent, I'm rich, so why am I condemned à la maison de mes parents?

[*Enter* EDWARD MORTIMER, *the father, age fifty, in a smoking jacket.*]

EDWARD. Good morning, dear. [*Kisses* CLARA.] Where is your mother?

VIOLA. She on a scabinger hunt. S–K–E–I–Z–B–R–T.

EDWARD. What?

CLARA. Viola says Mother went on a scavenger hunt last night, and I guess she's still there.

EDWARD. Is the Turkey with her?

CLARA. He's a Turk. And Mother doesn't like you to call him a turkey. His name is Abdhul, and he's a wonderful, handsome poet. And he unfortunately doesn't know I'm alive.

EDWARD. He's too busy living off of me.

CLARA. He's an artist!

EDWARD. That doesn't appear to have affected his eating habits any. Viola—what are you doing?

VIOLA. Ah'm eatin' chocklits.

EDWARD. Well, stop it. And serve breakfast.

VIOLA. Yassuh. [*Exits with box of chocolates, still eating.*]

EDWARD. There's no discipline in this house anymore.
[*Enter* ALLISON MORTIMER, *a fortyish scatter-brained rich lady in evening clothes, and her protégé,* ABDHUL, *who wears evening clothes and a turban.*]

ALLISON. Hello, children, we're home! And you'll never guess what—Abdhul and I won the scavenger hunt! You should have seen Dolly Adams, she was simply livid! We got absolutely everything. We got a goldfish bowl, and a goat—

EDWARD. And you already had a turkey.

ALLISON. I don't think that's funny, Edward. And then we found a ship's anchor, and a rose bush—oh, and then, Edward, guess what! Abdhul and I were the only ones to find an escaped prisoner from a chain gang—we found two!

CLARA. Mother!

ALLISON. Abdhul saw them, really. Tell them how, Abdhul.

ABDHUL. I see stripes.

ALLISON. That's right, he did. Dolly Adams was just green with envy.

CLARA. But what happened to the prisoners?

ALLISON. Oh, I forgot. I've asked them to breakfast. Abdhul, be an angel, and go bring them in. [ABDHUL *exits.*]

EDWARD. Allison, are you mad? Bringing two murderers into this house?
[VIOLA *sluffs in with plate.*]

ALLISON. We don't know that they're murderers, Edward. Maybe they're arsonists.

VIOLA. [*Putting plate in front of* EDWARD.] Heah are your eggs. [*Sluffs out.*]

EDWARD. Allison, I will not have you turn this house into a penitentiary.

ALLISON. Oh, Edward, eat your eggs.

CLARA. I think it's wonderful. I've never been in love with a criminal before.

ALLISON. Now, Clara, behave.

[ABDHUL *brings in the two escaped criminals—*
LORETTA *and* HANK. *They are both dressed in the
striped convict outfits.* LORETTA *looks extremely
upset and disoriented.* HANK *is tall and lanky,
seems uncomfortable in the rich home, but at-
tempts to carry it off with a down-home polite-
ness.*]

ALLISON. [*Being very cheerful.*] Well, here
   they are!

[EDWARD *looks away, reads his paper.*]

ALLISON. Now. Let me present my family.
   This is my husband, Edward Mortimer. [ED-
   WARD *doesn't look up.*] And this is my daugh-
   ter, the madcap heiress, Clara.

CLARA. Oh, Mother.

HANK. [*To* CLARA] How do you do, ma'am.

CLARA. I'm very pleased to meet you. Are you
   lovers who committed a crime of passion together?

ALLISON. Clara, don't be rude. They may not
   wish to discuss it. [*Enter* VIOLA, *carrying a
   plate.*] Oh, and this is Viola. I don't know her
   last name.

VIOLA. [*To* EDWARD] Heah's your English muf-
   fins. [*Sluffs out.*]

ALLISON. [*To* HANK *and* LORETTA] Now, what are *your* names?

HANK. My name's Hank, ma'am.

ALLISON. Hello, Hank. [*To* LORETTA] And you, dear?

LORETTA. My name's Loretta. [*Weeps.*]

ALLISON. Oh, forgive me, you must be famished. [*Takes plate of eggs from* EDWARD.] Give them your eggs, Edward. Viola will bring you more.
[ALLISON *gives eggs to* LORETTA.]

CLARA. [*Fascinated, to* HANK] What do you think of when you kill people?

ALLISON. Clara! [*To* HANK] You must excuse my daughter. She has a glandular condition.

HANK. That's all right, ma'am, but I've never killed anyone.

ALLISON. Good for you, Hank.

CLARA. [*Disappointed*] Well, why were you put on a chain gang, then?

HANK. I was falsely accused of robbing a grocery store in Tulsa, but I didn't do it.

CLARA. I've never been to a grocery store. What are they like?

HANK. I don't know. They're sort of small, they have food in them. . . .

CLARA. [*Enthusiastically*] But don't you just want to *kill* whoever sent you to prison unjustly?

HANK. No, ma'am. Even though American justice didn't work in my particular case, I still believe in it. [*Enter* VIOLA.]

ALLISON. The exception proves the rule. Isn't that so, Edward?

VIOLA. [*To* EDWARD] Heah's your oringe joose. [*Sluffs off.*]

EDWARD. Is there never to be a morning in which I can have all my breakfast at once?

ALLISON. Edward, please, your manners. [*Gives orange juice to* HANK.]

CLARA. [*To* HANK] Do you believe in destiny? I do. I believe it's my—

ALLISON. Clara, don't monopolize the guests. Abdhul, won't you favor our guests with one of your poems?

EDWARD. That does it! [*Throws down paper, starts to exit.*]

[*Enter* VIOLA *with plate of pancakes.*]

VIOLA. Heah's your wheat cakes.

EDWARD. [*Takes plate.*] You may send the syrup to my office!

[EDWARD *stalks out;* VIOLA *exits.*]

ALLISON. You must excuse Edward. He doesn't understand the artistic temperament. Abdhul, your poem.

ABDHUL. Ah! [*Rises, recites.*] Ganna tooey,
     Appasooft,
     Digannasuey la
      spleece,
     Swalla wimba
     Sreni vassa
     La breena zunu
     treest.

[*During above, enter* VIOLA *in hat and coat, carrying a bottle of syrup. She exits out front door with it.*]

ALLISON. Viola!

[CLARA *laughs; then so do* ALLISON *and* ABDHUL. HANK *and* LORETTA *look bewildered and out of place. Sound of happy-scene's-over music. In the midst of the laughter,* CLARA *pulls an unwilling* HANK *offstage, presumably to her playroom.*

LORETTA *looks anxiously after* HANK. ALLISON
keeps laughing the longest.]

ALLISON. [*To herself mostly*] Now, have I fin-
ished laughing? Yes. What should we do next?
Polo? Charades?
[*Doorbell rings.*]

ALLISON. Oh, good, the door. Now who could
it be? Well, it could be Dolly Adams, [*To*
LORETTA] or it could be the police for you, or
it could be the wealthy industrialist and his
wife I met at the scavenger hunt and who I
invited to breakfast.
[*Doorbell again.*]

ALLISON. Oh, the doorbell. Viola! [*Realizing*
VIOLA *is not there.*] Oh, could it *be* Viola? Loretta, could you get that for me?
[LORETTA *opens door. It reveals* JIMMY *and*
BETTE *dressed as Wallace Beery–Jean Harlow
social climbers now, instead of gangsters. Seeing
the still-alive* JIMMY, LORETTA *faints.*]

LORETTA. Jimmy! [*Faints.* JIMMY *tends to* LO-
RETTA. BETTE *seems surprised, but hasn't recog-
nized* LORETTA *yet.*]

ALLISON. Oh, dear. I'm so sorry. Good help is
hard to find these days.

BETTE. [*Trying to be grand.*] We get all our

domesticateds from the breadlines. And you get yours from the chain gang.

ALLISON. [*Slightly offended.*] Oh, well, Loretta is *substituting* for Viola.

BETTE. [*Upset hearing the name.*] Loretta . . . ?

LORETTA. [*Coming to.*] Jimmy! You're supposed to be dead.

JIMMY. Nah, they just nicked me a little. I been stayin' outta circulation 'til the heat was off, and then after Bette and I got hitched, I kinda drifted into big business.

LORETTA. [*Horrified*] Got hitched?

BETTE. Yeah. That's American slang for got married.

LORETTA. But I've been on a chain gang for killing you.

JIMMY. Gee, if I'd-a known, I coulda sprung ya.
[ALLISON *and* BETTE *are seated.*]

BETTE. [*To* JIMMY] Siddown.
[LORETTA *and* JIMMY *sit down.*]

ALLISON. [*Abruptly*] Well, why don't we all

have breakfast again? Abdhul, why don't you
whip up your thrilling soufflé?
[ABDHUL *nods and runs to the kitchen, laughing.*]

ALLISON. [*To* BETTE] It's a Turkish delicacy.

BETTE. Oh, I love exotic food. My husband and
I are goin' to the Alps for the Bavarian Cream
Pie.
[*Enter* VIOLA.]

VIOLA. [*Pleased*] I gave him the syrup.
[*Exits to kitchen.*]

ALLISON. That's Viola.
[*Enter* EDWARD, *carrying syrup and waffles.*]

EDWARD. [*Exasperated*] I can't go to the office
in my bathrobe.
[*Exits to bedroom.*]

ALLISON. And that's Edward.
[*Enter* VIOLA, *upset.*]

VIOLA. Mrs. Morrimer, you better come out
heah. Abdhul, he throwin' this, he throwin'
that. He gwine make a mess a my kitchen.

ALLISON. There is no such word as gwine.
Abdhul, dear!
[ALLISON *and* VIOLA *exit.*]

JIMMY. So how ya been, Loretta?

LORETTA. Jimmy, it wasn't supposed to turn out this way. It was all right to start out as an orphan, but then we were supposed to stay in Shanty Town and get married and always be happy.

JIMMY. Yeah, well, things turn out funny, don't they?

BETTE. I'm in the room too, ya know.
[ALLISON *rushes back in, in a splendid mood.*]

ALLISON. EVERYBODY! *Viola* is going to make breakfast, and *Abdhul* is going to imitate an ape. And after that we'll . . .

LORETTA. [*Standing*] I want this over.
[*Rings bell on wall.*]

ALLISON. Loretta, please, you're interrupting me.

LORETTA. You don't understand.
[*In response to the bell, enter the following:* HANK *and* CLARA *in party hats,* HANK *looking miserable and put upon;* EDWARD, *in the process of dressing for work;* ABDHUL, *who enters grunting and swinging his arms like an ape; and* VIOLA *with a cooking bowl.*]

LORETTA (Continued). I want it over. I HATE SCREWBALL COMEDIES!

ALLISON. [*Deeply offended*] Are you attempting to criticize our way of life?

LORETTA. You don't follow. I want the music to soar and the sign to come down and it can be *over*.

ALLISON. Edward, I think she's gone mad.

LORETTA. Please, you can do it. I'll show you. Look—Hank and Clara have fallen in love because they're screwballs and social class doesn't matter.
[LORETTA *pushes* HANK *and* CLARA *together.*]

HANK. I'm not a screwball.

LORETTA. And Jimmy marries . . . well, he can't marry me, so Abdhul marries me, and he becomes a lovable cardsharp who fleeces wealthy widows and I'm miserable for the rest of my life. . . . But Mr. Mortimer, on the other hand, is so happy that Abdhul is leaving his house that he takes Mrs. Mortimer over his knee and he spanks her. And we all laugh and laugh, and then the The End sign comes down and we don't feel anything anymore.
[*There is a long pause while* EVERYBODY *looks at* LORETTA *as if she's crazy.* LORETTA *seems relieved that she's discovered a way to end things.*

48

Suddenly the expressions on EDWARD, ALLISON, CLARA, *and* ABDHUL's *faces change, and they begin to act out what* LORETTA *has just described as if it were the most natural thing in the world and as if anything should be tried once.*

Throughout the following, HANK, BETTE, *and* JIMMY *look extremely bewildered and occasionally aghast.* JIMMY, *though, also seems to feel bad for* LORETTA.

EDWARD *now grabs* ALLISON, *puts her over his knee, and spanks her.*]

ALLISON. Edward, stop this! Stop it!!
[*Enter* VIOLA *with bowl and wooden spoon.*]

EDWARD. [*With* ALLISON *still over his knee.*] I'm not taking any more of your foolish behavior, Allison Mortimer. You bring home one more Turkey, or rajah, or any other foreigner in a turban, and you'll get a paddling from me you'll never forget.

VIOLA. Thash tellin' huh, Mr. Morimer.

ALLISON. [*Sternly*] Viola. [*Thrilled*] Oh, Edward, I've never *seen* you like this!

ABDHUL. [*Suddenly shuffling cards with great dexterity.*] Anyone for a friendly little game of poker? [*Gives* LORETTA *a hug.*]

CLARA. Oh, Mother, I'm so happy. At last I'm

in love too. [*To* HANK] And I hope when I'm bad, you'll spank *me*.

ALLISON. All my children are leaving the nest. [*Cries.*] I'm so happy.

VIOLA. [*To* ALLISON] Why, if Miz Clara is gettin' married, can Ah be a flower girl?

ALLISON. But, Viola, would you know how?

VIOLA. Sure. Ah knows all about flour!
[VIOLA *throws flour in* ALLISON's *face. Pause.*
EVERYONE *laughs:* VIOLA, CLARA, EDWARD, AB-
DHUL, ALLISON. LORETTA *looks possessed.* HANK,
BETTE, JIMMY *look very baffled and a bit alarmed.
There is extremely cheerful music, and the* THE
END *sign descends in front of the tableau. The
music crescendoes, finishes.* EVERYONE *holds the
scene; the laughter continues.*
*After a moment, the laughter stops, the music
has ended, and the* THE END *sign goes back up.
There is a long, uncomfortable silence.*]

BETTE. Perhaps we should go now.

ALLISON. [*Suddenly irate*] I will not allow the servants to behave this way. VIOLA! Go pack your things at once. We're sending you back to Georgia on the first available bus!
[VIOLA *exits, crying.*]

CLARA. Can we still get married?

ALLISON. CLARA—stop that. [*To* BETTE *and* JIMMY, *crossly*] Sit down.

[*They reluctantly do. Doorbell.*]

[*In a foul temper*] I suppose someone *else* has come to breakfast now. Loretta, do you think you could answer the door—*without* screaming this time?

[LORETTA *goes to the door, opens it. Enter* MICHAEL.]

MICHAEL. I'm looking for two convicts who've escaped from a chain gang.

[LORETTA *screams. She and* HANK *run.* MICHAEL *chases them, is tripped by* JIMMY. *Everyone exits, and we go to next scene.*]

Scene 10

Sirens begin. Frantic escape music. A large map of the United States is lowered and a spotlight focuses on Connecticut and moves with determination westward. Spot on HANK *and* LORETTA *running.*

The escape music changes to a romantic-tragic musical score, with sounds of people saying good-bye and of train whistles and steam. We hear voices say "Good-bye, Anna, good-bye." "Vronsky, Vronsky, don't leave me." "The train is almost here, Anna." "Vronsky, Vronsky . . ."

The map flies up, and in the upstage balcony we see DAVID *and* ERIC *staring out, watching the*

movie we hear. They are joined by LORETTA *and*
HANK, *out of breath.*

LORETTA. [*After a beat*] Do you think we
really have time to see a movie right now?

HANK. It's supposed to be real good. [*To* DAVID
and ERIC] What's happened?

DAVID. Well, Garbo's in love with Vronsky,
but things haven't worked out. . . .

ERIC. And she feels guilty that she hasn't been
a good enough mother to Freddie Bartholo-
mew. . . .

DAVID. And so she's at the train station and she
keeps looking down at the tracks as if she's
going to . . .

ERIC. . . . to jump.
[*The sound track's music becomes more tor-
tured; we hear the train start up, the rustle of
skirts, the train breaking to an abrupt stop, and
an awful scream. Then sad music.* LORETTA,
HANK, DAVID, ERIC *gasp.*]

ERIC. I didn't know they let people kill themselves in the movies.

LORETTA. They don't usually. Maybe because
it's in Russia.

[*The sad music is joined by the sound of blood-hounds.*]
Hank, do you hear dogs barking?

HANK. That's part of the music they play during the credits. No, I don't think it is. [*Starts to go; to* DAVID *and* ERIC] Is the next feature supposed to be good?

DAVID. Pretty good.

LORETTA. Hank!

HANK. You're right.

Scene 11

HANK *and* LORETTA *run out; escape music picks up; the map is lowered again, the spotlight stops somewhere around Oklahoma. The sound of dogs and escape music fades to that of wind and a melancholy harmonica.*

The map goes up; we see DAVID *and* ERIC *looking out at the next feature. Below them, lights up on* MA *and* PA JOAD, *staring out stoicly.* GRANDMA JOAD *lies dead in an old tire.*

PA JOAD. Ma, we got to bury Grandma.

MA JOAD. I wish Hank were here, Pa. Maybe he'll escape.

PA JOAD. Ya can't escape a chain gang, Ma.

MA JOAD. A Joad can, Pa. 'Cause We're the People, and you can't keep us down.

PA JOAD. Ya can't escape a chain gang, Ma.

MA JOAD. Look, here he comes now, Pa.
[*Enter* LORETTA *and* HANK, *out of breath and exhausted.*]

HANK. Ma!

MA JOAD. Hank boy! You're home.

PA JOAD. How'd ya escape, son?

HANK. Don't have time to talk. The bloodhounds'll be after us in a minute. Ma, this is Loretta.

MA JOAD. Welcome, Loretta.

HANK. Ma, where's the farm?

MA JOAD. There ain't no farm, Hank. They run us off and they razed it down.

PA JOAD. Dang bulldozers. Dang tractors.

MA JOAD. It's all right, Pa.
[SOUND: *of the bloodhounds again.*]

LORETTA. They're coming!

MA JOAD. Don't be afraid, honey. We're the People.

HANK. Ma, I'm gonna head me out for California. They say they got jobs in the movies for folks, Ma.

LORETTA. Please, we have to go.

MA JOAD. Hank, I don't wancha bein' in no movies, son. There's no life out there. You're too far from the soil.

HANK. I gotta try, Ma.

MA JOAD. Ain't ya gonna say good-bye, son?

HANK. Good-bye, Ma.
[SOUND: *bloodhounds somewhat closer.*]

MA JOAD. How am I gonna know about you, son, out there in the movies?

LORETTA. Please!

HANK. Well, maybe it's like Casey says, a fellow ain't got a soul of his own, just a little piece of a big soul. Then . . .

MA JOAD. Then what, Hank?

HANK. Then it don't matter. I'll be wherever ya look. Wherever there's a fight so hungry people can eat, I'll be there. Wherever there's a cop beating up a guy, I'll be there.

LORETTA. Please! Talk faster!

HANK. [*Talking faster*] I'll be in the way guys yell when they're mad, I'll be in the way kids laugh when they're hungry and they know supper's ready, and when people are makin' movies about the West and how this country got started, I'll be there too.

LORETTA. *Please!*

MA JOAD. [*Gives* LORETTA *a hard look.*] I don't understand it, Hank.

HANK. Gimme your hand, Ma. Good-bye.

MA JOAD. Good-bye, Hank.

HANK. Good-bye, Ma.

MA JOAD. Good-bye. [LORETTA *and* HANK *start to exit.*] *WAIT.* Hank, we ain't the kissin' kind but . . .

HANK. I'm gonna have to do a lot of it in the movies.

[*They laugh sadly at his joke, kiss. The* SOUND *of the bloodhounds abruptly stops.*]

LORETTA. [*Alarmed*] The barking's stopped!

MA JOAD. I don't hear nuthin'.

MICHAEL'S VOICE. [*Offstage*] Put your hands up or we'll shoot.

HANK. Loretta! Run! [HANK *runs. Much gunfire.* HANK *dies violently.*]

LORETTA. Hank!
[*Enter* MICHAEL. *He takes* LORETTA *into custody.*]

MICHAEL. Loretta Moran, you're under arrest. [*They take her out.*]

MA JOAD. [*Looks at* HANK *and dead* GRANDMA; *teary at first.*] Well, Pa, I guess he ain't gonna make no movies now. They're tryin' to break my will, but they ain't gonna do it. 'Cause We're the People. They can't wipe us out, they can't lick us. We'll go on forever, Pa, 'cause We're the People. [PA *starts to play his harmonica.*] Put that dang thing away, wouldja, Pa?
[PA *and* MA *look sadly at one another.*]

BLACKOUT

Scene 12

Ominous return-to-prison music. The SOUND *of a heavy prison door slamming shut. Lights up on* LORETTA *in prison.*

LORETTA. Oh, please, God, please. Don't leave me in prison for twenty-four years. Our Father, which art in heaven, hallowed be thy name . . . thy kingdom come, thy will be done . . .
[*As* LORETTA *continues to pray, offstage we hear the choral, stately singing of "O Come, All Ye Faithful."*
Spot on the PRISON WARDEN *(a woman). She takes out a sheet of paper.*]

PRISON WARDEN. I have good news for some of you girls. In honor of Christmas, I have governor's pardons for the following prisoners: Alice Adams, Susan Alexander, Crystal Allen, Esther Blodgett, Nora Charles, Stella Dallas, Norma Desmond, Helen Faraday, Dorothy Gale, Regina Giddens, Tess Harding, Fay La Rue, Tracy Lord, Rosa Moline, Loretta Moran, Mildred Pierce, Terri Randall, Sylvia Scarlett, Tootie Smith, Judith Traherne, and Florence Ziegfeld. I wish all of you girls the best of luck, and Merry Christmas.
[*During the above, when the* PRISON WARDEN *says* LORETTA's *name, the* BLESSED MOTHER *wafts in and stands, smiling, near* LORETTA; LORETTA

cannot see her, though. At the finish of the WAR-DEN's *speech, many* CAROLERS *in overcoats and mufflers, holding candles, enter singing "O Come, All Ye Faithful." A black and white* SANTA *rings a bell, and snow falls.*]

[*The* BLESSED MOTHER *graciously waves her hand, like the Ghost of Christmas Past, showing* LORETTA *the warmth and loveliness of the world.* LORETTA *smiles and is happy. Toward the end of the singing, she looks up, expecting the* THE END *sign to come down, although it does not.* LORETTA *is the last to exit, finally giving up on waiting for the sign.*]

Scene 13

Hollywood, the set of a Western. HANK *is dressed as a Gary Cooper–like cowboy;* EVE *is dressed in a frontier woman's dress; and the black actor plays an* INDIAN, *seated on the floor, motionless, wrapped in a blanket, with a couple of feathers in his head.*

MICKEY, *the newsboy of earlier in the play, is running around with a clapper board; and* DAVID *and* ERIC *are wandering through, looking with interest at the filmmaking proceedings.*

DIRECTOR. [*Over loudspeaker*] Everyone on the set for *Dobson's Pass.* Places, Mr. Joad, Miss Sheridan. [*Apparently seeing* DAVID *and* ERIC.] Mickey, we don't need extras for this scene. Send them over to wardrobe, we put them in *Clamdiggers*.

[MICKEY *hurries* DAVID *and* ERIC *off*.]

All right, lights. Camera. Sticks, Mickey.

[MICKEY *steps forward with a clapper board*.]

MICKEY. *Shoot-out at Dobson's Pass*, Scene 43, Take 88.

DIRECTOR. Action.

EVE. [*To* HANK] You can't go up there!

HANK. I gotta.

EVE. You can't. They'll kill you if you go up there.

HANK. I gotta.

EVE. What do you care if they kill Dakota Pete? What did Dakota Pete ever do for you?

HANK. Somethin'.

EVE. Well, what?

HANK. Somethin'.

EVE. Then I can't stop you?

HANK. Nope.

EVE. And you're gonna take on the whole Jenniper clan yourself?

HANK. Yup.

EVE. All right, go ahead, get killed, what do I care? You're insufferably monosyllabic, and I hate you. Good-bye.

HANK. G'bye. [*Walks out of the action; stands by the side.*]

EVE. Oh, I hate you, I hate you!

INDIAN. Why White Squaw squawk?

EVE. [*Crying*] I can't help it, I love him so much. . . .

INDIAN. Why White Squaw not soft like woman? Woman should be soft like fur of raccoon, woman should have babies. Why White Squaw not have babies?

EVE. [*Thinks, can't resist wisecracking.*] Well, I've been to the Stork Club *several* times, but nothing seemed to work out.

DIRECTOR. Cut!

MICKEY. Cut!

DIRECTOR. You speak to her, Mickey. I give up.

MICKEY. Miss Sheridan, that's not your line. Your line is "I want to have babies more than anything else, Chief Big Feather."

EVE. I know, but it's such a stupid line.

DIRECTOR. Miss Sheridan, if you ruin one more take with another one of these wise-cracks, you will find yourself back in the newspaper business faster than you can say Ben Hecht.

EVE. Oh, I never drop names.

MICKEY. [*Covering for her, before* DIRECTOR *can respond.*] *Shoot-out at Dobson's Pass,* Scene 43, Take 89.

DIRECTOR. Action.

EVE. [*Almost starts to laugh, collects herself.*] You can't go up there!

HANK. I gotta.
[*Enter* LORETTA, *dazed.*]

LORETTA. Help!

DIRECTOR. Cut! No visitors on the set, please.

HANK. Loretta!

EVE. Loretta Moran!

LORETTA. Hank!

HANK. I've been trying to contact you.

LORETTA. What happened?

HANK. Well, I was in the hospital for a while, but now I'm fine. I've been looking all over Hollywood for you.

LORETTA. You should have tried the prisons.

HANK. I didn't think of that.

DIRECTOR. I said no visitors.

HANK. [*Out to* DIRECTOR] Oh, please, Mr. von Leffing, won't you give her a job? She's a swell kid, and I know she has lots of talent, and she's had it so rough. Oh, please.

DIRECTOR. Very well, Mr. Joad. Put her in the next number.

HANK. Loretta, you're in. And if you work hard, I just know you're gonna succeed. Things are lookin' up for us, kid. [*Kisses her.*] Hey, Eve,

take her back to the dressing room and help
her learn the lyrics fast.

LORETTA. [*To* EVE] Which door do I use?

EVE. Well, there's the trapdoor, the humidor,
and the cuspidor. Which door did you want?

LORETTA. Oh, golly. [EVE *and* LORETTA *exit.*]
[HANK *removes his cowboy costume to reveal a
tuxedo.*]

DIRECTOR. Lights. Camera. Action.

MICKEY. *Clamdiggers of 1937*, Scene 107,
Take 2.

HANK. [*Sings*]

My favorite part of dinner
Is not the rich dessert.
Desserts don't keep you thinner,
Or bright-eyed and alert.
You may think that I'm crazy,
You may think my choice is pallid.
But once you see them all dressed up, you'll
know:
Why my favorite is the SALAD.
[*As* HANK *begins to sing the chorus of the song,
all the girls (including* EVE *and* LORETTA*) come
out dressed as vegetables in the salad: lettuce,
carrots, celery, etc. There is also a* CHEF, *and*
DAVID *and* ERIC *as* SALAD BOYS.]

HANK.

I love THE SALAD, I love THE SALAD,
I love to toss it up and pour the Roquefort on,
I love to eat the celery and the lettuce and the
  bean,
Cucumbers are the jokers, and a red tomato is
  the queen.
I love THE SALAD, I love THE SALAD,
I love to eat it up as you can plainly see,
I love THE SALAD, I love THE SALAD,
Won't you come dancing in the SALAD BOWL
  with me?

[*All the* GIRLS *come forward, Ziegfeld Follies
style.*]

GIRLS. [*Sing*]

We're in a SALAD, we're in a SALAD,
We've got a lot of what it takes to fill a bowl,
Bring vinegar and oil, French and Russian,
  Roquefort too,
As ladies of the SALAD, we have vegetation
  just for you,
We're in a SALAD, we're in a SALAD,
So whip out your salad fork and knife,
We're in a SALAD, we're in a SALAD,
Won't you come dancing in the SALAD BOWL
  OF LIFE?

EVE.
I want a honeymelon honeymoon,

A ripe banana crooning me a tune,
My Daddy says, "Absolutely nope,"
'Cause a grapefruit would be fine—but you cantaloupe.

LORETTA. [*Comes forward; she has to sing the pig Latin verse and seems a bit dazed.*]
Ere-way in-ay ALAD–SAY, ere-way in-ay ALAD–SAY,
Eve-way ot-gay ot-lay at-whay akes-tay oo-tay ill-fay owl-bay.

EVE. [*Spoken*] Good for you, honey.
[GIRL *comes forward as a sexy tomato.*]

GIRL.
I am a tomato, tomato, tomato,
Yes, I am a tomato, I'm red and I'm ripe,
The farmers who grew me, they all took right to me,
Yes, I am a tomato, I take dictation and I type.

HANK. You're hired! [*The* TOMATO *takes short-hand.*]
Take a letter. Dear Department of Agriculture, [*Spoken*]

> No more cakes,
> No more soup,
> No more ice cream,
> Not one scoop,
> Just one thing can make us sing:

ALL. SALAD, SALAD, SALAD, SALAD!

[*The* GIRLS *each speak solo lines in tempo.*]

GIRL 1.
I love radish,
Red and snappy,

GIRL 2.
Only lettuce
Makes me happy,

GIRL 3.
I love dressing,
Tart and sassy,

EVE.
I love God
And I love Lassie,

LORETTA.
I love blue cheese,

GIRL 1.
I love oil,

TOMATO.
Thousand islands
Rich and royal,

GIRL 2.
More than Garbo,

GIRL 3.
More than Gable,

GIRL 1.
I love SALAD
On the table.

ALL.
Salad, salad, salad, salad, SALAD, SALAD,
    SALAD, SALAD!
WE'RE IN A SALAD, WE'RE IN A SALAD,
So whip out your salad fork and knife,
WE'RE IN A SALAD, WE'RE IN A SALAD,
Won't you come dancing . . .
Won't you come dancing . . .
Won't you come dancing in the . . .

HANK. [*Out to* DIRECTOR] Do you like Loretta,
    Mr. von Leffing?

DIRECTOR. Finish the number, Mr. Joad.

HANK. But do you like her?

DIRECTOR. Very much. I think she's going to
    be a great star.
[*Everyone beams good-naturedly at* LORETTA.]

ALL. [*Finishing*] . . . SALAD BOWL OF LIFE!
[*The* THE END *sign majestically descends. Everyone holds pose.* LORETTA *notices the sign a bit
uncomfortably.*]

DIRECTOR. Cut. Okay, print it.
[THE END *returns up again.*]

DIRECTOR. Good work, kids. Places for the "Wrath of God" number. Mickey, get Dolores on the set.

[*Much moving about and exiting of* CHORUS.]

MICKEY. Miss del Reego, Miss del Reego, on set for "Wrath of God" number.

[*Enter* DOLORES, *an enormous fruit hat on her head.*]

DOLORES. Here I am, Fritz. [*Slips, falls to ground.*] Aggggh, who left this piece of lettuce here? Oh. Oh. MY LEG, MY LEG, MY LEG!

DIRECTOR. Okay, one of you kids in the chorus will have to take over the part.

EVE. Me, Mr. von Leffing?

DIRECTOR. You make too many wisecracks to be a star.

DOLORES. I can do the number, Fritz. It's just my leg.

EVE. You can't do the number with a broken leg.

DOLORES. Jes, I can.

EVE. You can't.

DOLORES. I can!

DIRECTOR. Ladies, ladies, Schweige doch! I want the new girl to do it, Loretta. . . .

DOLORES. But, Fritz . . .

EVE. [*Pleased for* LORETTA] Fritz . . .

DIRECTOR. Mickey, take the hat off Dolores. Take ten, everybody, while Loretta learns the part.

DOLORES. Fritz! [*To* EVE] How'd you like a piece of my mind?

EVE. Oh, I couldn't take the last piece.
[DOLORES *limps off in anger.*
MICKEY *brings back* LORETTA, *followed by* HANK *and* EVE. MICKEY *puts the fruit hat on* LORETTA.]

MICKEY. Here she is, Mr. von Leffing.

DIRECTOR. She doesn't look Spanish. Well, we make it a girl-next-door picture. Get the make-up artist. She needs a new name, something sweet. Mary. Polly . . . Pickford.
[MICKEY *brings on the* MAKEUP MAN, *who has wigs, eyebrows and several false noses.*]

Let me see some noses. Mary. Polly. Janet . . . Janet Gaynor. We'll call her Janet Gaynor.

MICKEY. Mr. von Leffing, we have a Janet Gaynor.

DIRECTOR. More noses.
[MAKEUP MAN *tries noses on* LORETTA *in quick succession; the discarded noses he throws on the ground;* EVE *keeps trying them on and looks out to* VON LEFFING *winningly with them.*]

Polly Gaynor. Mary Polly Janet Gaynor. Deanna Durbin. Deanna Janet Gaynor Durbin. I don't like that nose. Shave off her eyebrows.
[MAKEUP MAN *seemingly shaves off her eyebrows.* LORETTA *screams.*]

Mickey, go get a script from the trash bin for a screen test. Give her a wig, I see her as a sort of Janet Gaynor with a wig on. I like that nose. Cap her teeth. Does she have tonsils?

MAKEUP MAN. Yes, Mr. von Leffing.
[*Enter* ERIC, *followed by* DAVID. *Reenter* MICKEY *with scripts; he takes* LORETTA *aside, showing them to her.*]

DIRECTOR. Spray them. All right, ready for the screen test. [*Noticing* ERIC.] Who is this short person?

ERIC. They promised me a screen test too, Mr. von Leffing.

DIRECTOR. I am a very tall person. All right. Lights. Camera.

LORETTA. Am I supposed to be Spanish?

DIRECTOR. Action.
[LORETTA *is thrust into a test with* ERIC. *She is very monotone. She remembers some of the lines, peers at the script that* EVE *holds up for some of it, and makes up other parts.* ERIC *acts like a gangster.*]

LORETTA. I love you, Rhett Butler.

ERIC. Frankly, my dear, I don't give a damn.

LORETTA. But, Rhett . . .

ERIC. So long, sourpuss. [*Gives her a mock punch on the jaw as* JIMMY *does.*]

LORETTA. [*Reminded of* JIMMY.] I'll win him back. After all, tomorrow is . . .

DIRECTOR. Cut! Stinks! Give her a bus ticket, Mickey. Him too.
[MICKEY *gives* LORETTA, *then* ERIC, *a bus ticket.*]

MICKEY. Tough luck, Miss Moran. Sorry, fella.
[DAVID *and* ERIC *exit.*]

LORETTA. [*To* HANK *about* ERIC] He reminded me of Jimmy a little.

EVE. Aw, he ain't worth it, kid. No man is.

LORETTA. I guess I better catch that bus. [*Dazed*] Good-bye . . .

HANK. Don't go, Loretta. I want to marry you.

LORETTA. I can't get this nose off, Hank.

HANK. It would make Ma real glad if we got married, Loretta.

LORETTA. Don't pull the nose so hard, Hank. I'd like to make your mother happy, Hank, but . . . Leave the nose alone, try the eyebrows. . . . It's just that I'm afraid I still love Jimmy, I can't get him out of my mind. . . . [*Cries.*]

HANK. Loretta, please marry me.

EVE. I'll marry you, Hank. [*She perhaps still has a false nose on, too.*]

HANK. Why are you crying, Loretta? Are you unhappy you can't get your nose off?

LORETTA. It's not that, Hank. It's just that sometimes I don't think the thirties are ever going to be over. [*Exits, crying.*]
[*Citizen Kane–like music—brooding and ominous—is heard; and we go to the next scene.*]

Scene 14

Lights up on BETTE, *well dressed, sitting on the floor, doing a large jigsaw puzzle.* JIMMY *sits far away from her, stern, brooding.*

BETTE. There are too many pieces to this puzzle. And it's all sky anyway. Six million pieces of blue cardboard. I'm gonna go crazy. [*Pause.*] Ain't you talkin' anymore?

JIMMY. I was thinking of someone.

BETTE. Who?

JIMMY. Finish your puzzle, Elizabeth.

BETTE. *Her* again?

JIMMY. Shut up. You got what you wanted, you're a big shot in society, so shut up.

BETTE. Okay, I wanted to be successful, ain't I allowed? But you—you overdo everything. You run five newspapers, two auto factories, a glue works, two senators, all those so-called nightclubs; you started the Spanish-American War, for God's sake. All you do is achieve, achieve, achieve. IT'S NEUROTIC!

JIMMY. Practice your singing, Elizabeth.

BETTE. And that's another thing. I DON'T WANNA BE NO OPERA SINGER!
[JIMMY *starts to choke her, won't stop. Enter* HARKNESS, *their butler.*]

HARKNESS. Sir. Sir.
[JIMMY *stops his choking.*]

HARKNESS. Sir, I have the information you wanted on the whereabouts of that certain person.

JIMMY. Where is she, Harkness?

HARKNESS. She left Hollywood several months ago, sir. The agency has traced her to—I'm sorry to say—the Club Intimate.

JIMMY. I see. That will be all, Harkness.

HARKNESS. Yes, sir. [*Exits.*]

JIMMY. I've got to see her.

BETTE. Please, not now, Jimmy. I need help with the Italian pronunciation.

JIMMY. Ito can help you with *Tosca.*

BETTE. Ito is Japanese.

JIMMY. Practice your singing, Bette. *Sing.*

[*Chokes her again; she has to sing a scale with his hands around her throat.*]

BLACKOUT

Scene 15

In blackout, we hear the SOUND *of a piano tinkling. Lights up on* PIANO MAN, *an amiable black man playing the piano.* JIMMY *sits at a small side table.*

PIANO MAN. [*To the room at large, show about to start*] Hi, everybody, this is Piano Man, welcoming you back to the Club Intimate and reminding you all to be real nice to our pretty hostesses. And now the Club Intimate is happy to present, back from a month of drying out in White Plains, Lady Loretta from Room 779. Let's have a big hand for the little lady, and don't nobody buy her a drink. [*Enter* LORETTA *in slinky nightclub garb.*]

LORETTA. Oh, my God. Is this the hospital?

PIANO MAN. Just sing, honey. Piano Man'll tell you where you are later.

LORETTA. Okay. [PIANO MAN *plays introduction; she doesn't come in.*] Excuse me. I have something in my ear. [*Knocks side of her head; introduction again.*] I'm sorry, I can't quite hear the piano. Would someone buy me a drink?

[PIANO MAN *looks sternly at the audience. No one offers.* LORETTA *starts to cry.*]

LORETTA. Oh . . . I . . .

JIMMY. [*Outside of spotlight*] I'll buy the lady a drink.

LORETTA. [*Can't see straight.*] Thank you, whoever you are.

[JIMMY *brings her a drink from his table. She gulps it right down.* JIMMY *returns to his table.*]

Mmmmmm, that was delicious. I think I'll try again, Piano Man. [PIANO MAN *plays introduction. This time she sings.*]

EUPHEMISM FOR SALE,
What am I bid for my Whatchamacallit?
EUPHEMISM FOR SALE,
What does it matter what people call it?
I'm just a ship in a storm,
I need a captain to keep me warm,
Drop your anchor—if you're male,
I've got a EUPHEMISM FOR SALE.

I'm traveling down a certain road
That's forbidden by the Production Code.
My name's Taxi, stay awhile,
I don't charge for—the first mile. . . .

EUPHEMISM FOR SALE,
What am I bid for my Whosamadoosey?
I get sent through the mail,
Special rate for a fourth-class floozie.
I like to play by the sea,
Hey little boy there, please play with me,
You've got the shovel, I've got the pail,
I've got a EUPHEMISM FOR SALE,
What am I bid for
My EUPHEMISM FOR SALE?

JIMMY. [*Calls to her*] Loretta.

LORETTA. Have I stopped singing?

JIMMY. Hey, sourpuss. Don't you know me?

LORETTA. Your voice is familiar. Are you the one who gave me the black eye?

JIMMY. Loretta, it's Jimmy.

LORETTA. [*Not comprehending*] Jimmy, Bobby, Harry, the Mayor. Buy me another drink, huh, baby?

JIMMY. You shouldn't drink, kitten.

LORETTA. But I have to do such awful things, and I mustn't remember them, and ... there's someone I have to forget. *His* name was Jimmy. [*Realizing it's* JIMMY *in front of her*]

Oh, Jimmy. [*Cries.*] Our vines have such tender grapes. [*Pause.*] Can I have some wine?

JIMMY. No more, kid. We gotta get you well. Hey, Piano Man, play "Shanty Town Romance." [PIANO MAN *does.*]

LORETTA. [*Hearing song*] Oh, Jimmy—let's go back to Shanty Town.

JIMMY. We don't need Shanty Town, sourpuss. I got ambition. I'm runnin' for governor, I'll be elected tomorrow. And then after that I'll be President, and after that . . .

LORETTA. I want Shanty Town. I want it to be raining and for you to sing that song, and then for The End sign to come down and then we can stay frozen behind it forever.

JIMMY. Ya can't have that, kid.

LORETTA. Can I drink?

JIMMY. No more.

LORETTA. Can we go to the movies, then?

JIMMY. Not now. Howd'ya like to see a really bad opera?
[*They look at one another. We hear* BETTE'S *singing of scales. Lights dim on their looking at one another.*]

Scene 16

Backstage at the opera. At left is BETTE's *dressing room; she is behind a screen making singing noises. With her is her houseboy* ITO *(played by black actor).*

MICKEY *is running around, being efficient.* DAVID *and* ERIC *in opera peasant garb are about.*

MICKEY. Fifteen minutes, everybody. Come on, let's get this turkey on the road. [*To* DAVID *and* ERIC] Opera peasants stage right, please.

DAVID. Who's that singing?

MICKEY. That's the star.
[DAVID *and* ERIC *hold their noses, shake heads, exit right.* MICKEY *goes to* BETTE's *dressing room area.*]

MICKEY. Fifteen minutes, Mrs. O'Reilly. [*Exits.*]

BETTE. Oh, my God. [*Comes from behind screen; she is dressed as Brünnhilde.*] I still don't know the Italian. Say something Italian, Ito.

ITO. Nooky nooky.

BETTE. Don't say that, Ito. It's annoying. [*Enter* MICKEY.]

MICKEY. Here's a note from your husband, Mrs. O'Reilly. And ten minutes. [*Exits.*]

BETTE. You read it, Ito.

ITO. Good ruck on your opening. So solly you cannot sing. Am divorcing you to mally Loletta, she plegnant with my baby. Hope you choke on own spit. Jimmy.
[*Enter* MICKEY.]

MICKEY. Two minutes, Mrs. O'Reilly.

BETTE. You just said ten minutes.

MICKEY. Times flies when you're having fun. [*Exits.*]

ITO. Why you dressed this way? That not right for Tosca.

BETTE. I don't know what I'm doing!
[*Enter* MICKEY.]

MICKEY. Places! [*Exits.*]

BETTE. What is the matter with him? Ito, before I go on, find Loretta in the audience. And tell Harkness I want a gun.

BLACKOUT

Scene 17

SOUNDS *of orchestra tuning up.*
Lights up in "opera box" (right balcony); seated are ALLISON *and* CLARA MORTIMER. *Enter* JIMMY *in evening dress, looking for* LORETTA.

JIMMY. [*To* ALLISON] Hey, you seen Loretta?

ALLISON. Oh, Mr. O'Reilly, how nice. You remember my daughter, the madcap heiress Clara.

CLARA. [*On edge*] Mother! You have *got* to stop saying that.

JIMMY. [*Calling*] Loretta!

ALLISON. Ssssh.
[*The opera begins. Enter a gypsy peasant, perhaps* HANK.]

HANK. [*Sings*]
Ostende nobis, Tosca,
Ostende nobis, Tosca,
Hip, hip, oremus!
[*Enter* BETTE *as Brünnhilde, dragging* LORETTA, *who's bound and gagged.* BETTE *is brandishing a gun madly.*]

BETTE. [*Sings*] Ho-yo-to-ho! Ho-yo-to-ho!

[BETTE *shoots the gun in* JIMMY's *direction. He and* CLARA *duck.*]

ALLISON. I love Verdi. He *begins* with climaxes.

BETTE. [*Occasionally singing, but more often addressing the audience*] You must not vote for my husband for governor.

JIMMY. This isn't *Tosca*, Bette.
[*Enter* DAVID *and* ERIC *as opera peasants.*]

DAVID and ERIC.
Hic, haec, hoc,
Huius, huius, huius,
Hic, haec, hoc,
Huius, huius, huius . . .

BETTE. [*Shoots at* JIMMY.] You must not vote for him. He shares a love nest with an alcoholic floozie.

JIMMY. Sing, Bette.

BETTE. I love you, I love you! [*Sings*] Je t'aime, Jimmy!
[*Shoots at him;* ALLISON *dies.*]

CLARA. Mother!

BETTE. I'm going to kill Loretta, Jimmy.

[*Enter* HARKNESS. *The performance comes to a halt.*]

HARKNESS. Excuse me for interrupting the performance, madam. I must speak with you.

BETTE. What *is* it, Harkness?

HARKNESS. Madam. They've bombed Pearl Harbor.

BETTE. Who has?

HARKNESS. The Japanese, madam.

BETTE. Why?

HARKNESS. I don't know, madam.

BETTE. Oh.

HARKNESS. This will mean war, madam.

BETTE. Well, I presume so.

HARKNESS. I've taken the liberty of firing Ito, madam. We've placed him in a camp.

BETTE. Very good. Thank you, Harkness. [HARKNESS *exits.*] [*To audience*] Well, you have all heard Harkness. The United States is at war. [*Exits.*]

LORETTA. [*Being untied by* JIMMY.] Jimmy, what's going to happen?

JIMMY. I can think of one thing.

LORETTA. What?

JIMMY. I'm going to enlist. —
[*A sudden flurry of activity. Everyone runs every which way—to get out of costume, to enlist, etc.* CLARA *sees* MICKEY *as he runs by.*]

CLARA. [*Calls to him*] Hey! Please, don't leave me. My mother's dead and I need you.

MICKEY. But I don't even know you.

CLARA. Funny things happen during wartime. I love you.

MICKEY. You're a funny kid. [*They kiss.*]

CLARA. Oh, Mickey, I don't understand what the war's for.

MICKEY. I do. It's so that a little kid in Kansas can grow up on a farm and be President or senator or dogcatcher or whatever he wants to be. It's for that lady with the light, it's for the Fourth of July and the Declaration of Independence. It's so that a young girl like you can be free to buy herself an ice cream soda in a soda shop in Vermont.

CLARA. I'm hungry. [*They kiss. Drum roll.*]
[*Lights come up on an enormous American flag in black and white. It falls away to reveal a dazzling color flag in red, white, and blue sparkles. The play has switched to color. EVE enters, dressed as the Statue of Liberty.*]

EVE. [*Sings*]
You've got to take a stand,
You've got to lend a hand,
So pack your gear, as thousands cheer,
Go march off to that band.
[*All the men march in in uniform—Army, Navy, etc. All women stand on side to wave them on. JIMMY is in the forefront. LORETTA runs up to him.*]

LORETTA. Be careful, Jimmy.

JIMMY. Don't worry, sourpuss.

LORETTA. What should I do about the baby?

JIMMY. Name him Jimmy.

LORETTA. All right, Jimmy.
[*Enter BETTE.*]

BETTE. I'm pregnant also. What would you like me to call *my* baby? Have you any suggestions, Loretta?

LORETTA. No.

JIMMY. Well, I have. I want you both to put aside your differences until this war is over. Because we all have to act as one nation now because whatever these babies are called it's for them we're gonna be fighting. We're all Americans.

LORETTA. [*Waves.*] Good-bye, Jimmy.

ALL [*Sing, marching in place*].
We've got to . . .
Nip the Nips in the bud,
Zap the Jap and spill his blood,
Rout the Kraut, wipe him out,
Chop Hitler into sauerkraut,
If we are really men,
It's war again, world war again,
It's a great world war again.

EVE and WOMEN.
So raise your voice, increase your stride,
We have Roosevelt and God on our side.

ALL.
America is number one,
We are never number two,
And over there we're gonna win,
For the red and white and blue!
[*The men march off. The women wave good-bye.*]

END ACT I

ACT TWO

Scene 1

Lights flash, sound of explosions. JIMMY, *in his Army uniform and helmet, is writing a letter. Near him is* MICKEY, *also in uniform and helmet.* MICKEY, *terrified of the bombs, shivers and whimpers throughout scene.*

JIMMY. Dear Sourpuss. Tomorrow I am going on a dangerous mission behind enemy lines. I don't know if I'll get back alive. But if I die I will die for a good cause. I realize now that when I killed people in the early 1930s, it was wrong because it was done for selfish reasons, for personal gain. However, I find that my years as a gangster were an excellent training for dealing with these stinkin' Nazis. Shootin' Joe Ferruchi and seein' his head roll about in a plate of spaghetti has prepared me for the worst these Nazis can dish out. Even the memory of settin' Fadder MacNeil on fire . . . [*Annoyed at* MICKEY'S *whimpering,* JIMMY *suddenly shoots his gun at* MICKEY, *who screams.*] Look, kid, you don't quit the crybaby stuff,

I'm gonna aim better next time, got me?
[MICKEY *nods.*] What's your name, kid?

MICKEY. Mickey.

JIMMY. Well, keep it down, Mickey. [*To himself*] Kids. War ain't for kids.

MICKEY. [*Softly*] No . . .

BLACKOUT

Scene 2

Lights up on EVE, *dressed as a Wac. With her is* LORETTA.

LORETTA. Eve, what can I do to help the war effort?

EVE. [*Lifts up* LORETTA'*s skirt, points to* LORETTA'*s leg.*] See that? Hitler's afraid of that.

LORETTA. Oh, Eve, you're joking.

EVE. I never joke anymore. You wanna help our boys? Come to the Canteen tonight and bring those gams with you.

LORETTA. [*Thinks.*] The Canteen ... [*Lights fade.*]

BLACKOUT

Scene 3

In blackout above, we hear the sound of forties big-band dance music. Lights up on small area with CLARA *in a fluffy school-dance kind of dress. She comes up to* DAVID, *chewing gum and wearing some sort of uniform. Band music keeps on in background.*

CLARA. You wanna dance, Soldier?

DAVID. No thanks.

CLARA. My boyfriend's overseas. His name's Mickey.

DAVID. Uh huh.

CLARA. Actually he's my husband. We only had one night together. My mother got shot at the opera.

DAVID. Oh yeah?

CLARA. [*Kisses him passionately.*] That's for

Mickey, wherever he is! [*Kisses him again, long.*] I'm an emotional wreck. [*They kiss passionately.*]

[*Enter* EVE *in her Wac uniform. She salutes.*]

EVE. Good evening, soldiers of the United States military forces, and welcome to the Home-Away-from-Home Stage Door Hollywood Canteen, Lieutenant Eve Sheridan reporting. [*Sees* CLARA *kissing.*] You've met our hostesses, and now meet our entertainment!

[*Enter* LORETTA *and* BETTE *wearing only lingerie. Catcalls.*]

EVE. You said it!

LORETTA.
Keep your chin up
With a PRETTY PINUP,
She will keep her chest up,
And you can keep the rest up.

BETTE.
Keep your chin up
With a PRETTY PINUP,
While you're in the action,
Let her give satisfaction.

LORETTA.
Just think of Grable and her legs,
And you can scramble Hitler's eggs.

BETTE.
If Rita Hayworth makes you hot,
That's one more Nazi who gets shot.

LORETTA, BETTE and EVE.
Keep your chin up with a PRETTY PINUP,
Keep your chin up, G.I. Joe.
[CLARA, *who has been watching from side with*
DAVID, *suddenly takes off her dress.*]

CLARA. This is for Mickey! [*Joins* LORETTA *and
the others.*]

EVE.
Betty has her legs,

LORETTA.
And Lana has her sweater,

BETTE.
Rita Hayworth's mouth
Is like a mouth but wetter,

ALL FOUR.
Our patriotic duty lies
In keeping up our legs and thighs. . . .

Keep your chin up
With a PRETTY PINUP,
You make Hitler's knees shake,
We will give you cheesecake.

We won't make you have to beg,

We'll show some bust and then some leg,
Keep your chin up,

> CLARA. I love you, Mickey!

With a PRETTY PINUP,

> LORETTA. I love you, Jimmy. Keep your chin up.

Keep your chin up,

> BETTE. [*Mad at* LORETTA] I love you, Jimmy.

> CLARA. I love you, Mickey!

With a PRETTY PINUP,
Keep your chin up, G.I. Joe!

> CLARA. I'm a wreck.

BLACKOUT

Scene 4

SOUND *of explosions. Back to* JIMMY *writing his letter.*

JIMMY. . . . and Loretta, if I should be killed tomorrow on this dangerous mission that I mentioned earlier in the letter, I want you to know how proud I am that you've become a pinup girl. And I know the little guy inside of you will be, too, when he arrives on the scene. I've got to stop writing now, Loretta. The dawn is beginning to creep up over the hillside, like old Landlord Death come to collect his final rent. . . .

BLACKOUT

Scene 5

Backstage at the Canteen. LORETTA *reading* JIMMY's *letter to* EVE.

LORETTA. . . . I've got to stop writing now, Loretta. The dawn is beginning to creep up over the hillside, like old Landlord Death come to collect his final rent. . . .
[*Enter* ERIC *dressed as a telegraph boy.*]

ERIC. Telegram, Miss Moran.

LORETTA. Oh. [*Looks at it, faints.*]

EVE. [*Reads it.*] James T. O'Reilly. Missing in action.

ERIC. Gee.

EVE. And her about to have a baby. It's not fair.

BLACKOUT

Scene 6

MICHAEL O'REILLY *and* DAVID *in a couple of movie house seats, staring out at the screen, presumably having been watching the preceding telegram scene on the screen.* MICHAEL *has been watching the screen since the beginning of the act; and* DAVID *joined him after the "Pinup" number.*

DAVID. How do you like this picture?

MICHAEL. Watching a weeping woman for two hours is not my idea of a good time.

DAVID. What's your idea of a good time?

MICHAEL. My idea of a good time is fearing God and honoring my country and keeping fit in mind and body. Sometimes I think that's why women don't like me the way they like my brother Jimmy. So I've memorized three humorous stories. Would you like to hear them?

DAVID. Oh, I'd love to hear them.

DAVID. Oh, I'd love to hear them. Yes, but maybe we should wait till after the war is over.
[*They go back to watching the screen.*]

Scene 7

SOUND: *of a baby crying at birth; a slap. Lights up on* LORETTA, *propped up with pillows in a chair, recuperating.* EVE *by her,* HANK *stands holding flowers.* EVE *is holding the baby, showing it to* LORETTA.

EVE. It's a fine, healthy-looking boy, Loretta. What are you going to call him?

LORETTA. [*Pause.*] Missing in action. [*Cries.*] [*Everyone looks disturbed. Lights dim.*]

BLACKOUT

Scene 8

SOUND: *of a baby crying at birth, again; a slap. Lights up on* BETTE, *propped up with pillows in a chair, recuperating.* VIOLA, *the colored maid of the Mortimers, has become a nurse and is holding a baby.*

VIOLA. You give birth to your baby jus' fine, Miz O'Reilly.

BETTE. Let me see it. [*Looks at it; grimly*] Did you do something to this baby?

VIOLA. No, Miz O'Reilly. Ah didn't do nothin'.

96

BETTE. This baby is Japanese.

VIOLA. Yassum.

BETTE. That damn Ito! [*Pause.*] What about Loretta's baby? Is it Japanese?

VIOLA. No, ma'am. Miz Loretta's baby looks jus' like Mr. O'Reilly.

BETTE. I'm sick of always coming second to Loretta. Sick, do you hear me?

VIOLA. Yes, ma'am. Ah hears you.

BETTE. Give me a piece of paper. [VIOLA *does;* BETTE *writes.*] Dear Miss Loretta Moran, the United States Army regrets to inform you that Mr. James T. O'Reilly, previously reported as missing, has been found dead. Our regrets, signed General . . . [*Thinks.*] Douglas MacArthur. [*Folds the paper.*] I'm going to find my husband and win him back if I have to join the military to do it. Viola, send this telegram to Loretta and send this baby to a camp.

VIOLA. Yassum. [*Exits with baby and telegram.*]

BLACKOUT

Scene 9

LORETTA's *hospital room again.* LORETTA *is depressed and staring off.* EVE, HANK *still with flowers. Baby is in bassinet.*

HANK. Eve, I've never seen her this depressed.

EVE. Hank, I'm going to talk to her. [*Goes closer to* LORETTA.] Loretta, listen to me. I've watched you for the last ten minutes. I've seen how you've lain here in bed and you haven't touched that child once. Do you know what you are? You're a quitter. That's right, a quitter. You're full of self-pity, self, self, self. Well, I don't feel sorry for you. You know why? Because you have a baby, and you have a career as a pinup girl, and if Jimmy is alive, you'll have a husband, and even if he's dead, at least you will have been loved! Who do you think you are to feel sorry for yourself? Jane Froman doesn't have the use of her legs, but do you see her carrying on this way? No! She's out entertaining the troops on crutches. Where are you? Where would the Allies be if they acted the way you do? [*Tears in her voice.*] Well, I don't feel sorry for you because you're nothing but a quitter! [*Cries, hides her face in* HANK's *shoulder.*]

LORETTA. Thank you, Eve. I feel strong again. And Hank, how nice you've become a priest.

HANK. Well, when I couldn't get into the Army to fight this war, I thought I should fight another kind of war. His war.

EVE. Oh, brother.
[*Enter* ERIC.]

ERIC. Telegram for Miss Moran.
[LORETTA *looks worried, reads telegram. Pause. She screams, faints, dropping the baby along the way.*]

EVE. [*Takes telegram.*] The United States Army regrets to inform you . . . [*Looks at* HANK.] He's dead, Hank. [*Looks at* LORETTA.] Poor kid. [*Sees baby.*] Pick up the baby, Hank.

HANK. [*Picks it up.*] The baby's dead.

EVE. Well, there's the trapdoor, the humidor, and the cuspidor.

HANK. Cut it out, Eve.

EVE. You're right, Father.

BLACKOUT

Scene 10

At the movies. A few chairs, facing out to the "screen." Seated are LORETTA, *a* WOMAN PATRON, *and* VICTOR HENREID, *a suave European in his forties. We hear the* SOUND TRACK.

WOMAN (on sound track). Oh, John, I love you more than I love skating!

MAN (on sound track). But, darling—why not love me *and* skating?

WOMAN (on sound track). You mean—you don't mind? Oh, John, let's skate forever!
[*On the* SOUND TRACK *the music soars cheerfully, and there is the sound of skating on ice. These skating sounds should continue until indicated.* LORETTA *has been crying throughout above.*]

PATRON. Sssssh. Ssssssh. Why are you crying? This picture is a comedy.

LORETTA. I hate skating.

PATRON. Then you shouldn't have come to this picture.

LORETTA. I hate skating, and I hate John. And the Nazis made me drop my baby, and I hate the Nazis. I HATE THE NAZIS. I HATE THE NAZIS.

PATRON. Sonja Henie is not a Nazi.

LORETTA. She sounds like she is. And she's not

doing anything to stop them. What do the Nazis care whether she skates or not? I HATE THE NAZIS.

[*The* SOUND TRACK *crescendoes, the skating stops, the picture's over.*]

PATRON. I am going to report you to the manager. [*Exits.*]

VICTOR. [*To* LORETTA] I could not help overhearing you. My name is Victor Henreid.

LORETTA. You don't sound American.

VICTOR. I am Austrian. I hate what the Nazis have done to my country. I am a member of the Austrian underground. I am on my way to Tunis. Would you like to help us?

LORETTA. My life is worth nothing to me. If it can be worth something to the underground . . . why not?

VICTOR. [*Lights two cigarettes in his mouth, offers her one.*] Cigarette?

LORETTA. I'm sorry, I don't smoke.

VICTOR. You will have to learn. May I be your teacher?

[SOUND TRACK *starts again; sounds of music and skating.*]

VICTOR. On our way to Tunis we must stop at Casablanca to get letters of transit. Shall we go?

LORETTA. Wait. I missed the beginning. [LORETTA *sits down, watches the movie.* VICTOR *does likewise, smokes his two cigarettes.*]

BLACKOUT

Scene 11

A café in Casablanca. PIANO MAN, *the black from the Club Intimate, is there at the piano, playing a Hoagy Carmichael–like song. With him is* JIMMY.

PIANO MAN. How's your amnesia today, Mister Rick?

JIMMY. Fine, Piano Man. I ain't remembered nuthin' since I came to Casablanca eight days ago.

PIANO MAN. You come here six months ago, Boss. Why you come to Casablanca, Boss?

JIMMY. I came to Casablanca for the waters.

PIANO MAN. But there ain't no waters here, Boss. [*Laughs.*] I know, you wuz misinformed.

[*They laugh.*] You use that line a lot, don'tcha, Boss?

JIMMY. Stick to your piano playin', why don't-cha? [PIANO MAN *starts to play* "*Shanty Town Romance.*"] Don't play that one.

PIANO MAN. Why not, boss?

JIMMY. I dunno. Just don't play it.
[*Enter* BETTE *and* MICHAEL *in their military uniforms.*]

MICHAEL. [*To* BETTE] And then the Moron says, "But I *am* a chicken."

BETTE. Stop telling me that joke. I hate it.

MICHAEL. Major O'Reilly, you can't keep looking for Jimmy all over Europe.

BETTE. Yes I can, Major O'Reilly.

MICHAEL. You'll never find him.

BETTE. [*Sees* JIMMY] James!

MICHAEL. Oh no.

JIMMY. You lookin' for somebody?

BETTE. James, it's me! Your wife.

JIMMY. [*Truly not recognizing her*] You tell her, Piano Man.

PIANO MAN. Mister Rick here has amnesia, ma'am. He don't remember nuthin'.

BETTE. [*Looks at them both as if they're crazy.*] But you've got to remember. I'm your wife. [*Points to* MICHAEL.] This is your brother. You tried to make me an opera singer. Don't you remember? [*Sings*] Ho-yo-to-ho!

MICHAEL. Major O'Reilly, keep a hold of yourself.

BETTE. Perhaps it's my uniform. I wasn't alway a Wac, James. I used to do big puzzles. You used to hit me.

JIMMY. Look, I got a lousy memory about dames. Beat it.

BETTE. JAMES, I'M YOUR WIFE!

JIMMY. Have a grapefruit!
[JIMMY *pushes a grapefruit in her face, goes to a table and has a drink.* BETTE *has hysterics.*]

MICHAEL. [*To* JIMMY] That was a rotten thing to do. [*To* BETTE] Are you all right?

BETTE. I have a seed in my eye. [MICHAEL checks her eye.]

[*Upstage enter* LORETTA, *looking lovely. No one sees her right away except for* PIANO MAN. PIANO MAN *plays "Shanty Town Romance."*]

JIMMY. [*Violent*] I thought I told you never to play that!

LORETTA. Jimmy! [*He looks at her.*] You're alive. . . .

JIMMY. [*Looks at her; his amnesia leaves.*] Your name is sourpuss. My name is Jimmy. It's 1943.

PIANO MAN. That's right, boss!

JIMMY. I remember everything.

BETTE. [*Sees* LORETTA.] Oh no.

LORETTA. Jimmy, I didn't know you were alive.

JIMMY. I'm American, ain't I?
[*Enter* VICTOR. *He goes up to* LORETTA, *kisses her.*]

VICTOR. I'm sorry to take so long, darling. I was afraid the hatcheck girl was a Nazi.

JIMMY. Who's this Bozo?

LORETTA. Jimmy, this is my husband, Victor
    Henreid.
[BETTE *looks up hopefully.*]

VICTOR. How do you do? [*Puts out his hand.*]

JIMMY. Your what? [*Pause.*] I'll kill him! [*Goes
    to hit* VICTOR.]

LORETTA. Jimmy, don't hit him! He's a mem-
    ber of the underground. [VICTOR *looks an-
    noyed;* LORETTA *realizes she's let out a secret.*]
[JIMMY *starts to punch* PIANO MAN.]

JIMMY. I thought I told you to stop playin' that
    lousy song. Ya dumb head! [JIMMY *continues
    to beat up* PIANO MAN. *All else look embar-
    rassed.*]

BETTE. I love you, James. Hit *me*. Hit *me*.

JIMMY. [*Finished with* PIANO MAN.] I'm takin'
    this here bottle and I'm gonna drink it until
    I get amnesia all over again.
[JIMMY *exits with his bottle.* BETTE, crying, is
taken off by MICHAEL.]

LORETTA. I'm sorry he hit you like that, Piano
    Man.

PIANO MAN. That's all right, Miss Loretta. He hurtin' inside.

LORETTA. We all are, Piano Man.

PIANO MAN. You white folks like me to play somethin' to cheer you up?

VICTOR. Do you know the "Marseillaise"?

LORETTA. Oh, not now, Victor. I have the most awful headache.

VICTOR. Very well. We only have a few minutes before the plane leaves. [*Gets an odd look in his eye.*] Excuse me, I must check something. [*Exits.*]

LORETTA. Play it, Piano Man.

PIANO MAN. But I doesn't know the "Marseillaise," Miss Loretta.

LORETTA. [*Smiles sadly.*] Play it. [PIANO MAN *starts to play "Shanty Town Romance." Singing*] Di di di di di di di di di di . . .
[*Shot offstage. Enter* VICTOR.]

VICTOR. The hatcheck girl *was* a Nazi. I had to kill her.

LORETTA. Yes, Victor.

VICTOR. Killing is wrong, Loretta. I want you to understand that. Do you remember when I read Victor Hugo's *Les Misérables* to you aloud and how I said it was wrong for a man to steal bread, but how the world itself was wrong where a man had to steal bread to feed his family?

LORETTA. Yes, Victor. I remember. The book was a trifle long, I thought.

VICTOR. Killing Nazis is like stealing bread, Loretta. It is wrong, but it must be done until the world is a just one.

LORETTA. You better dispose of the bread, Victor.

VICTOR. Yes, you're right. [*Pause.*] That man with amnesia. He meant something to you once, didn't he?

LORETTA. Who? Mr. O'Reilly? [*Laughs hilariously.*] Really, Victor, you are too much. Go bury the Nazi and I'll practice smoking.
[VICTOR *exits.* LORETTA *practices. Reenter* JIMMY.]

JIMMY. I've come to say good-bye to you and your dull husband before your plane leaves.

LORETTA. Victor is a wonderful man. He's good and noble, he's everything you're not, but it's true—I am bored to death with him! Oh, Jimmy, I don't want to get on the plane to Tunis with him. I don't want to read any more Victor Hugo. Jimmy, let's run away together. [*They kiss.* PIANO MAN *starts to play* "*Shanty Town Romance.*"] You'll have to think for both of us, for all of us.

JIMMY. All right, I will.
[SOUND *of the plane.*]

LORETTA. The plane. Oh, Jimmy, I'll never leave you again.

JIMMY. You have to, sourpuss. If that plane leaves the ground and you're not on it with him, you'll regret it. Maybe not today, maybe not tomorrow, but soon and for the rest of your life.
[PIANO MAN *begins to play the theme very dramatically and loudly.*]

LORETTA. What about us?

JIMMY. We'll always have Shanty Town. But I've got a job to do, too. And where I'm going, you can't follow; what I've got to do you can't be any part of.

LORETTA. Don't play it now, Piano Man. I can't concentrate.

JIMMY. Loretta, I'm no good at being noble, but it doesn't take much to see that the problems of three little people don't amount to a hill of beans in this crazy world. Someday you'll understand that.

LORETTA. What about beans? [*Very upset*] I don't want you to play now!

JIMMY. Here's looking at you, sourpuss.
[*Enter* VICTOR.]

LORETTA. Here's looking at me? What does that mean? Are you confusing me with someone else?

VICTOR. Loretta, dear, the plane for Tunis is waiting.

LORETTA. What about Tunis? I haven't heard a word anyone has said.
[VICTOR *and* LORETTA *exit.*]

JIMMY. That didn't go the way I wanted.
[PIANO MAN *stops playing. Sound of plane take-off. Enter* BETTE *and* MICHAEL.]

BETTE. Did you tell her good-bye?

JIMMY. Yeah.

BETTE. Good. Now you have two alternatives.

You can tell me you love me and I can tear up these orders—or you can reject me and be sent on an extremely dangerous mission and probably be killed. Which is it to be?

JIMMY. Gimme the orders.

BETTE. Very well. No hard feelings. I hope you die in that mission. I hope your eyes shrivel up and fall out of your head. I want you to know that I love your brother. I'm divorcing you and marrying your brother right after we invade Normandy. Forget I said anything about Normandy, I'm a wreck. Kiss me, Michael. [MICHAEL *and* BETTE *kiss;* BETTE *runs out.*]

MICHAEL. She's very high-strung, but militarily quite brilliant.

JIMMY. [*Looking at his orders.*] Now, what about this bomb I'm supposed to drop?

MICHAEL. Well, it's very powerful, and if all goes well we have hopes of its bringing this war to a close. Now, your first target is Hiroshima. Now, what you need to know is that the atom is the smallest particle of matter which has the characteristic chemical properties of an element. There are three fundamental subatomic particles: the proton . . .

JIMMY. Michael, I have a feeling this is the beginning of a beautiful friendship . . .

MICHAEL. . . . having unit positive charge and mass number 1; neutron, having neutral charge and mass number 1; electron . . .
[*Lights fade on* JIMMY *and* MICHAEL *walking off. The* THE END *sign is lowered. Sounds of an enormous, long explosion. The* THE END *sign shakes considerably, goes up again.*]

BLACKOUT

Scene 12

In blackout we hear the music of the following song. Lights up on Three Forties Singers singing in front of a radio microphone like the Andrews Sisters. (They are normally EVE, BETTE, *and a third actress,* ALLISON *or* MA JOAD.)

THREE SINGERS.
Well, we got ourselves an APPLE BLOSSOM VICTORY,
And they're ready with confetti Maine to Tennessee,
Gonna learn to live with the atomic bomb,
Cause it's back to God and apple pie, and back to Mom,
Come home, boys, come home to your wives,
These are the best years of our lives. . . .

Welcome ba-ack,
Welcome ba-ack,
   You were there at Iwo Jima,
   You flew over Hiroshima,
   You're a hero in khaki,
   You destroyed Nagasaki,
   And we'll never drop another,
   But if we should drop another:

EVE.
Don't sit under the atom bomb with anyone else
   but me. . . .

THREE SINGERS.
Welcome back,
It's an APPLE BLOSSOM VICTORY!
Za-ba-da-ba-do-bop-bop, yeah!
[*Enter* LORETTA *and* VICTOR.]

LORETTA. The war is over, Victor.

VICTOR. Yes, Loretta.
[*Various soldiers return, including* DAVID, *greeted by* ERIC.]

LORETTA. The soldiers are coming home now,
   Victor.

VICTOR. Yes, Loretta. We are entering a new
   decade. It will be called the postwar decade.
   It will be a period of building up, of restoring.
   There will be a baby boom. The forces of

right have won in their struggle, and much
will be accomplished in the coming years.
[*Enter* MICKEY *and* CLARA *from opposite sides.*]

CLARA. Mickey!

MICKEY. Clara!

CLARA. I've been promiscuous!

MICKEY. I have no hands! [*Holds up his hand-
less arms.*]
[MICKEY *and* CLARA *run together and embrace.
Enter* EVE *and* FR. HANK.]

EVE. The war is over, Hank. Everyone's come
home.

HANK. Yes, Eve.
[*Enter* MICHAEL. *From other side, enter* BETTE.]

MICHAEL. Bette!

BETTE. Michael! [*They embrace, kiss.*]

EVE. Everyone's kissing, Hank.

HANK. Yes, Eve.

EVE. Do you ever give up celibacy, like for
Lent?

HANK. Celibacy is a serious thing, Eve.

EVE. I love you, Hank. [*Kisses him.*]

HANK. You shouldn't have done that, Eve. [*Exits.*]

EVE. [*Calling after him*] Don't worry. You can always get a tetanus shot. [*Exits after him.*]

MICHAEL. Bette. It's good to see you.

BETTE. It's good to see you. Who are you?

MICHAEL. I'm your husband, Michael.

BETTE. Jimmy is my husband.

MICHAEL. Jimmy is your ex-husband. I'm his brother.

BETTE. I married his brother? Why did I do that?
[*Enter* JIMMY, *back from the war.*]

BETTE. Jimmy!

MICHAEL. [*Holding her back.*] I'm your husband now, Bette. [MICHAEL *pulls* BETTE *offstage.*]
[*Enter* LORETTA *and* VICTOR. LORETTA *sees* JIMMY.]

LORETTA. [*Clutched throat.*] Jimmy!

JIMMY. Loretta. [*They face each other, do not embrace.*]

LORETTA. You remember my husband, Victor?

JIMMY. How ya doin'?

VICTOR. Well, thank you. And yourself?

JIMMY. Okay.

LORETTA. How is your wife, Bette?

JIMMY. She married my brother, Michael. I'm free now, Loretta.

LORETTA. Oh. You remember my husband, Victor?

VICTOR. I understand that you were the pilot who dropped the atom bomb.

LORETTA. Oh, did you do that, Jimmy?

VICTOR. I have great hopes that atomic energy will be used for the general betterment of mankind in the coming postwar years.

LORETTA. Victor's full of hopes. It makes him fun to be with. [*Cries.*]

VICTOR. Loretta, Liebchen, did I say something wrong?

LORETTA. No, Victor. Something's flown in my eye.

JIMMY. Lemme see if I can get it out. [JIMMY *takes* LORETTA *a few steps away from* VICTOR.] Meet me at the Club Intimate in an hour, and we'll talk about killin' this dodo for his insurance.

LORETTA. Jimmy, we couldn't.

JIMMY. I dropped the bomb, didn't I?

LORETTA. I know, but that was mass slaughter, this would only be killing one man.

JIMMY. You love me, don'tcha? Meet me in an hour.

VICTOR. Liebchen, we'll be late for the concert.

LORETTA. Yes, Victor. [*To Jimmy*] We're very fond of Schubert.
[LORETTA *and* VICTOR *exit.*]
[*Reenter* BETTE; MICHAEL *follows after her.*]

BETTE. Yoohoo, Jimmy, I'm here! [*Smiles.*]

JIMMY. Oh yeah? Drop dead.

MICHAEL. [*Grabs a hold of* BETTE.] You'll learn
to love me, Bette.

BETTE. Yes, I'm sure I will.
[BETTE *gets an uncontrollable facial tic; then
turns on* MICHAEL *and beats on his chest hysterically.*]

MICHAEL. Bette! Do you think you should see
a psychiatrist?

BETTE. Yes, maybe I should. [*Facial tic re-
turns.*] What's a psychiatrist?
[BETTE *is dragged off struggling by* MICHAEL.
CLARA *and* MICKEY *break from their embrace.*]

MICKEY. How promiscuous were you?

CLARA. Well, how much of your hands are you
missing?
[*The* THREE SINGERS, *now* TWO SINGERS—*minus*
BETTE—*return and hum portions of* "*Apple Blossom Victory.*" *Their singing is interrupted by a
startling intrusion of eerie, science fiction music.
Lights change.* CLARA, MICKEY, JIMMY, *and perhaps the* TWO SINGERS *all watch.*]
[*Upstage, enter a* ROBOT, *all silver. His voice
comes over the speaker system, not from himself.*]

ROBOT. People of the planet Earth. I have
come with a warning to you from the planet

Zabar. My name is Edward. Beware atomic power, people of earth. Within it you hold the possibility of destroying the entire universe, including Zabar. Already the deadly radiation emanating from the first atomic explosion is killing thousands of people in Japan. People who have been near this deadly radiation may have mutant children or, among the male species, find themselves sexually impotent. If you have been near atomic radiation, go to a doctor at once. I am from the planet Zabar. You must join the United Nations. My name is Edward. [*Exits.*]

CLARA. [*Screams hysterically.*] AAAAAAAAA AAAAAAAAAGGGGGGGGGHHHHHHHHHH .... Mickey, what did he mean?

MICKEY. I don't know.

CLARA. You've never been near the atom bomb, have you?

MICKEY. No, never.

CLARA. Thank goodness.
[JIMMY *has overheard them, looks worried.*]

CLARA. It's so terrifying. AAAAAAAAAAAAA AAAAGGGGGGGGGGGHHHHHHHHHH!

BLACKOUT

Scene 13

The Club Intimate. PIANO MAN *playing "Shanty Town Romance."* JIMMY *sits by him.*

JIMMY. Piano Man, if you had a friend who loved a woman but he couldn't marry her because he had been near some nuclear power or something, and he'd been to a doctor and the doctor said he couldn't, well, this person couldn't be a man anymore, well, if you were this friend, what would you do?

PIANO MAN. I'd kill myself.

JIMMY. [*Considers it.*] But if you didn't do that, what would you do?

PIANO MAN. Why, I'd send myself back to Africa.

JIMMY. Look, you keep playin' that song, I'm gonna break your hands. [PIANO MAN *stops.*] Play somethin' else.

PIANO MAN. Okay, Boss. [*Plays "As Time Goes By."*]

JIMMY. [*Scribbles on a piece of paper.*] Piano Man, When Loretta comes, give her this note. And now—good-bye. [*Exits.*]
[*Enter* LORETTA.]

LORETTA. Piano Man.

PIANO MAN. Good to see you, Miss Loretta.

LORETTA. Is Jimmy here yet?

PIANO MAN. He done left you a note. [*Gives her the note.*]

LORETTA. [*Reads it.*] But all it says is "Good-bye."

PIANO MAN. I guess it ain't meant to be, Miss Loretta.

LORETTA. But it's so ... terse. [*Cries. She gulps down a drink from the piano.*] Pour me another one, Piano Man.
[PIANO MAN *looks worried. Lights dim.*]

Blackout

Scene 14

HANK, *a drunk* LORETTA, EVE, CLARA, *and three other people at an Alcoholics Anonymous meeting. They stand in line.* EVE, HANK, *and* LORETTA *are numbers 5, 6, and 7 respectively.*

PERSON 1. My name is Wally Marvin, and I am an alcoholic.

EVE. Good for you, Wally, that's an important step.

LORETTA. [*Drunk*] Where are we, Gustaf?

HANK. Don't be afraid, Loretta.

PERSON 2. My name is Elizabeth Purtridge, and I am an alcoholic.

LORETTA. I gotta get outa here. These people are drunks.

HANK. You can't keep running away, Loretta.

PERSON 3. My name is Daniel Goldman, and I am an alcoholic.

HANK. God'll help you, Loretta.

LORETTA. No, He won't. He doesn't like me.

CLARA. My name is Clara Myrna Mortimer, and I am an alcoholic.

LORETTA. They're getting closer.

EVE. My name is Eve Sheridan, and I am an alcoholic.

HANK. I pass. Your turn, Loretta.

LORETTA. I pass.

HANK. You can't keep running away, Loretta.

LORETTA. I can, I can!

HANK. Say your name.

LORETTA. I don't remember it.

HANK. Say it after me, my name is Loretta . . .

LORETTA. My name is . . .

HANK. Loretta . . .

LORETTA. My name is nobody and I'm not anything. [*Runs out.*]

EVE. Well, you tried, Father. I guess she wasn't ready.

PERSON 1. I bet she goes out and has a drink.

PERSON 2. What does she drink mostly, Father?

HANK. I don't know really.

PERSON 2. I wonder if she likes scotch.

PERSON 1. I never liked scotch. I liked bourbon a lot, though.

BLACKOUT

Scene 15

Fifties saxophone music. A street. LORETTA *drinking from a bottle.*

LORETTA. This is the bottom. Hello, bottom, hello. [*Cries.*] It's the war really. When the war was on, none of us had time to be neurotic. But now that it's over, there's just all this time. . . . [*Cries.*]

[*The* BLESSED MOTHER *appears, dressed in blue. Supernatural music.*]

BLESSED MOTHER. Loretta.

LORETTA. Oh, God, the D.T.'s.

BLESSED MOTHER. Loretta, don't turn away from God. I'll intercede for you.

LORETTA. I'm afraid.

BLESSED MOTHER. Don't be afraid. Did you see *The Song of Bernadette* with Jennifer Jones?

LORETTA. Yes, Your Grace.

BLESSED MOTHER. She wasn't afraid. And what happened to her?

LORETTA. [*Confused and crying*] She won an Oscar.

BLESSED MOTHER. That was during the war. To win an Oscar now, you must overcome great personal difficulties. Do you think you can do this?

LORETTA. [*Standing.*] I want The End sign to come down and I want to stay frozen behind it.

BLESSED MOTHER. Loretta, do you have faith enough in God and in yourself to overcome polio?

LORETTA. But I don't have polio.
[*The* BLESSED MOTHER *waves her hand, and* LORETTA *falls down, stricken with polio.*]

BLESSED MOTHER. Find the strength within yourself, Loretta. It's within yourself. . . . [*Disappears.*]

LORETTA. No, don't leave me, no . . . no. . . .
[*Music. A platform is pushed on by* DAVID *and* ERIC *in tuxedos. Enter* MICKEY, *dressed up for an awards ceremony and holding an Oscar under his arm.*]

VOICE. And now the Academy presents the next major award of the evening.

MICKEY. The nominations for Best Actress are: Bette O'Reilly as an unhappily married woman still in love with her former husband, Jimmy, but fast forgetting him due to several rounds of shock treatments in *Love Me or Leave Me in the Snake Pit.*

[*Applause. Enter* BETTE *in an evening gown. She has a completely blank stare and has to be helped to her place by* ERIC. *She doesn't seem to know where she is.*]

Eve Sheridan as an alcoholic spinster shamefully in love with a Catholic priest and fast finding her wisecracks unable to protect her from an empty bed in *Losing Her Sense of Humor.*

[*Applause. Enter* EVE *in an evening gown. She is led to her place by* DAVID *and seems glum indeed.*]

Clara Mortimer as a dimwitted socialite who can't cope with her husband's losing his hands in the war in *We the Victors.*

[MICKEY *looks self-conscious on* We the Victors. *Applause. Enter* CLARA *in an evening gown.* ERIC *leads her to her place; she holds his hand too long, and he has to pull it away.*]

Loretta Moran as an alcoholic ex-ingenue who must overcome polio in *I'll Cry with a Song in My Heart Tomorrow.*

[*Applause.* LORETTA *waves.*]

And the Blessed Virgin Mary in *Sunset Boulevard.*

[*Applause. Enter the* BLESSED MOTHER.]

And the winner is . . . [*Tries to open the envelope, can't.*] . . . Clara, would you help me with this? [CLARA *does.*] . . . LORETTA MORAN!

[*Applause.* CLARA *gracefully applauds; the* BLESSED MOTHER *is perhaps bitter, up to the actress;* EVE *is glad for* LORETTA; BETTE *tries to applaud but has trouble getting her hands to hit one another.*]

[LORETTA *drags herself with great difficulty over to* MICKEY *and the Oscar.* EVE *eggs her on with encouraging "You can do it, come on," etc., type statements. As courageous background music soars,* LORETTA *manages to get to her feet and to stand and walk once again. Tears stream down her face. The applause is immense.*]

LORETTA. [*Weeping, holding the award.*] I am . . . so deeply grateful. I haven't really even made a movie, and yet you have given this to me. If only we can find our way again —maybe we can; through the courageous stories of recovery of people like myself or Lillian Roth or Marjorie Lawrence or . . .

[JIMMY, *in a leather outfit like Brando's in* The Wild One, *stumbles in, drunk.*]

LORETTA. . . . oh.

JIMMY. Congratulations. . . .
[*Everyone onstage is embarrassed for* LORETTA.]

LORETTA. Hello, Jimmy. You're wearing leather.

JIMMY. I'm a Rebel.

LORETTA. What are you rebelling against?

JIMMY. [*Thinks.*] What've ya got? [*Laughs; moves drunkenly; accidentally knocks her in the mouth.*] I'm sorry, I'm always hurting people. I just killed this old woman with my motorcycle out front. . . . [*Cries.*]

LORETTA. Don't cry, Jimmy. . . .

JIMMY. I don't mean to be bad.

LORETTA. None of us do.

JIMMY. I dropped the bomb, but now there's no place for me to fit in.

LORETTA. Maybe we'll have to drop the bomb again. . . .

MICKEY. I'm sorry, we have to give the next award now.

JIMMY. [*Really violent*] Don't hassle me. [*Shakes him.*] You understand me. Don't hassle me!

CLARA. Please, don't hurt him, he hasn't any hands!

MICKEY. Will you shut up, will you just shut up!

LORETTA. Oh, this is all so public, I can't stand it.

JIMMY. Loretta, I'm impotent. Will you marry me?

LORETTA. Please, we can't talk here. Everyone's listening. Come on, Jimmy.... [*Starts to lead him off.*]

CLARA. [*Crying with* MICKEY.] Don't forget your Oscar....

LORETTA. [*Taking it.*] Thank you. I'm sorry you didn't win.

CLARA. Please, just go away. [*Trying to get it out.*] The next award is the Jean Hersholt Humanitarian ... [*Can't get it out; weeps, holds* MICKEY; LORETTA *and* JIMMY *exit weeping.*]

[CLARA *and* MICKEY *exit, distraught; likewise* EVE *and the* BLESSED MOTHER. *Only left onstage are* BETTE, *still staring blankly, and* DAVID *and* ERIC. *The* VOICE *tries to get the award show going again.*]

VOICE. And now Eve Sheridan will sing the next nominated song, "Isn't It Fun to be in the Movies," from the film "Seven Brides for Twelve Angry Men."

[*Music begins, but* EVE *is too upset, and exits, crying.*]

VOICE. The song will be sung by the Blessed
   Virgi . . .
[*The* BLESSED MOTHER *mysteriously mouths "no,"
and wafts out.*]

VOICE. . . . by Bette O' . . . [*Under his breath*]
   Ernie, is there anyone backstage who's around
   who could sing . . . don't talk to me about union
   problems now . . .
[*The music keeps vamping. Onstage are* BETTE,
still staring blankly; and DAVID *and* ERIC. *After a
bit* DAVID *and* ERIC, *to cover, start to sing the song.
After a bit, they relax into it, and should be
neither bitter nor fake happy.*]

DAVID and ERIC.
Isn't it fun to be in the movies,
Way up there on the screen,
Isn't it great us actin' like smoothies,
If you know what I mean,
Once we were sitting down there below,
Now we're up here, and we're part of the show,
Isn't it fun, us gettin' our kicks,
Makin' 'em laugh in Hollywood flicks,
Rollin' and reelin' along. . . .

Isn't it fine to be in the movies,
Ain't it peachy and keen?
Queue up in line, and come see a movie,
Yes, tonight, Josephine,
Once we were sitting down there below,
Now we're up here, and we're rarin' to go,

Isn't it fun, we're happy as loons,
Kickin' our heels and singin' some tunes,
Rollin' and reelin' along. . . .

The fifties are fraught
With problems, I know,
Still we can cope,
'Cause ain't it impressive
Our problems look bigger
In CinemaScope,
Todd-AO, Todd-AO. . . .

Isn't it fun to be in the movies,
In that flickering light,
Twenty to one you'll see in the movies,
What you dreamed of last night,
Once we were sitting, popcorn in hand,
Now we're up here, and we're leadin' the band,
And isn't it great, we feel in the pink,
Our lives are in shambles, but we're still in synch,
Rollin' and reelin',
Cause that's how we're feelin',
Just rollin' and reelin' along. . . .

[DAVID *and* ERIC *bow;* BETTE *sort of nods her head too. We hear a foghorn, leading to the next scene.*]

Scene 16

A rooftop. The sounds of foghorns and sea gulls. JIMMY, *still in leather, stands by* LORETTA, *who is in her slip.*

LORETTA. Why are we on this rooftop, Jimmy?

JIMMY. Well . . . Hoboken ain't much but . . . I call it home.

LORETTA. It's so ugly. [JIMMY *cries*.] Don't cry, Jimmy.

JIMMY. You don't unnerstan'. I coulda been a contender, I coulda been somebody.

LORETTA. We'll move away from here. We don't have to stay in Hoboken. We'll go back to Shanty Town.

JIMMY. What are you talking about? This is Shanty Town.

LORETTA. What do you mean?

JIMMY. This is where it was. Right here in Hoboken.

LORETTA. I don't believe you. This isn't Shanty Town. It isn't. You're lying to me.

JIMMY. I swear to God, sourpuss. It's the truth.

LORETTA. [*Looks out.*] I remember it differently.
[JIMMY *puts his arm around her, and they walk out, sadly.*]

BLACKOUT

Scene 17

A gavel. The House Un-American Activities Committee. MICHAEL *is behind a desk. A* PRISON MATRON *is present. Seated is* MA JOAD. *With her are* FR. HANK *and* EVE.

VOICE. [*Stern; serious; underneath him we hear FBI movie music—serious, patriotic*] October 26, 10:44 a.m. A committee room in the Congress of the United States. Within these walls, the fate of democracy as we now know it may be decided.

HANK. Be strong, Ma.

MA JOAD. I ain't afraid, son. We're the People.

MICHAEL. Name.

MA JOAD. Ma Joad.

MICHAEL. Age.

MA JOAD. I'll be one hundred and two this Febr . . .

MICHAEL. Now, Mrs. Joad, are you now or have you ever been a member of the Communist Party?

EVE. You don't have to answer these questions, Mrs. Joad.

MA JOAD. I'm a Democrat.

MICHAEL. Mrs. Joad, you were heard to say by a witness friendly to this committee—your son—the phrase "We're the People."

HANK. I'm sorry, Ma. I felt I had to.
[EVE *and* MA *look at* HANK *in shocked surprise.*]

MICHAEL. What did you mean by that phrase?

MA JOAD. It don't mean nothin'. It's just a little somethin' I say to raise my spirits a little.

MICHAEL. Did it ever cross your mind that it might raise the spirits of the *Russian* people a little?

MA JOAD. I didn't say it in Russian.

MICHAEL. Mrs. Joad, I have here a needle-point pillow bearing the aforementioned phrase, "We're the People." [*Holds up red pillow.*] Do you deny having made it?

MA JOAD. [*Cheerfully*] No. I love it.

MICHAEL. Do you deny it's *red*?

MA JOAD. [*Agreeably*] No, it's red.

EVE. Don't answer any more of these questions, Mrs. Joad. They're idiotic.

HANK. Eve, this isn't your place.

MICHAEL. There aren't going to be any more questions. Mrs. Joad, if we don't execute you, the next thing we know you'll be needlepointing *state secrets* to the Communists.

EVE. Execute!

MA JOAD. But I don't know no state secrets.

MICHAEL. We only have your word for that, don't we? Guilty as charged. [*Bangs gavel.*]

VOICE. [*Heard as we watch* MICHAEL *exit; music in background again*] October 26, 11:20 a.m. Michael O'Reilly moves on, ever watchful for treason and sedition. He knows that the Communist Menace must not go unchecked if the Garden of our Liberty is to flourish and grow.

MA JOAD. Why'd you do it, Hank?

HANK. Ma, we have to stop communism somewhere.

MATRON. It's time now, Mrs. Joad.

MA JOAD. No, I don't want to die. I want to live.

HANK. Come, Ma, let's pray.

MA JOAD. I ain't gonna pray. I'm gonna scream. [*Screams horribly.*]
[MATRON *drags off* MA, *who continues to scream and scream.*]

VOICE. Even now the eyes of Soviet agents may be on some of you, looking for dupes. Be on guard, and take heed of men like the courageous Fr. Hank Joad—men ever on the alert to halt the Red Menace.

HANK. I mean, she did say it. We're the People. She said it all the time.

EVE. I've wasted a lot of time being in love with you, Hank.

HANK. Eve, don't go now.

EVE. So long, Hank. [*Exits.*]
[SOUNDS *of an electrocution and a flashing light come from offstage. A spot hits* HANK's *face.*]

HANK. Ma! Ma! [*Rips off his priest's collar.*] Ma's dead! Ma's dead!

BLACKOUT

Scene 18

At the movies. Several chairs facing out. The following people sit together: BETTE *and*

MICHAEL; CLARA *and* MICKEY; EVE *by herself;*
HANK *by himself (holding Ma's pillow);* STUART,
a black man, by himself.

MICHAEL *is in his military uniform.* BETTE *looks
odd. She has on a blond wig, lots of red lipstick,
and a tight dress which has been awkwardly
padded to suggest an extremely ample figure.
She should look something like Marilyn Monroe,
but it should not be too exact. It should look
like the attempt of a crazy person to look like
Monroe. She should purse her lips a lot, like
Monroe.*

On the SOUND TRACK *we hear the music to what
sounds like a biblical epic. The music should
continue on until almost the end of the scene,
though at a low and, hopefully, unobtrusive
level.*

Toward the end of the scene, the BLESSED
MOTHER *comes into the theater to watch the
movie too.*

VOICE OF GOD. These are the Ten Commandments. Honor the Lord thy God. Thou shalt have no molten images.

BETTE. [*Southern accent, like Monroe's in* Bus Stop] What's a molten image?

MICHAEL. Bette, why are you talking in that accent?

BETTE. I'm talkin' about what's a molten image.

MICHAEL. Be quiet, Bette.

VOICE OF GOD (on sound track). Thou shalt not take the name of the Lord thy God in vain. Keep holy the Sabbath.

BETTE. Is that Esther Williams?

MICHAEL. No. That's Charlton Heston.

BETTE. You told me Esther Williams was going to be in this.

MICHAEL. I didn't, Bette.

BETTE. You did.

EVE. [Annoyed] Sssssssssssh.

BETTE. [Hurt] Sssssssssssh y'self.

VOICE OF GOD. Honor thy Father and thy Mother. Thou shalt not kill.

BETTE. I'm tryin' to sound like Kim Novak in Picnic. Actually she didn't talk that way. It's more like Marilyn Monroe in Bus Stop. Do you think I look like her? Maybe I'm Carroll Baker in Baby Doll.

EVE. Will you be quiet?

BETTE. I'm tryin' to be quiet, if you'd all just quit hushin' me.
[*Enter* LORETTA, *by herself; sits alone.*]

LORETTA. [*Sings*] It's that ol' Black Magic, that ya hear so well . . .

MICHAEL. [*Furious*] When you pull yourself together, I will be at the Strategic Air Command. I hope you pass through this period of your life. I find it very depressing. [*Exits.*]

EVE. [*To both of them*] Shut up!

BETTE. [*Calling sadly*] Hey! Oh well.

LORETTA. Is that Bette?

BETTE. Who's that?

LORETTA. [*Moving over.*] It's Loretta.

BETTE. Oh, hi, honey! You come to the movies?

EVE. I am going to get the manager! [*Exits in a huff.*]

LORETTA. I'm married to Jimmy now.

BETTE. That's nice.

LORETTA. You look different.

139

BETTE. Do I? Well, I bleached my hair. Or maybe it's a wig. [*Takes off her wig; looks at it.*] No. I bleached it. You look different, too.

LORETTA. I know. I feel different. I feel like I'm in a Lana Turner movie about adultery.

BETTE. Oh, I love those. I don't know what movie I'm in. [*Cries.*]

LORETTA. I want to commit adultery.

BETTE. [*As if she heard a question*] Oh, I'm fine. I'm a member of the Joint Chiefs of Staff now. Ever since we had Hank Joad's momma executed.

LORETTA. Hank. He always found me attractive, I think. Do you know where he's living now?

BETTE. Over there. [*Points to* HANK *in theater.*] [LORETTA *moves over next to* HANK.]

LORETTA. Hello, Hank. It's Loretta.

HANK. Ssssssh, I'm watching the movie.

LORETTA. You're not a priest anymore, I see.

HANK. No. Uh, I left.

LORETTA. I have an unhappy marriage, Hank. I want to commit adultery.

HANK. Uh . . . [*Smiles, nervous.*]

LORETTA. I always thought you loved me, Hank.

HANK. Well . . .

LORETTA. I always liked you, ever since we first met on that chain gang. A lot's happened, Hank. Why are you fidgeting so much?

HANK. Uh, I dunno. Uh, Ma was just sayin' the other day that I'm too shy with girls.

LORETTA. [*Taken aback*] Hank. Ma is dead.

HANK. What?

LORETTA. Hank, Ma is dead.

HANK. No she ain't. Ma ain't dead. Are you, Ma? [*Speaks in a falsetto voice for "Ma."*] No, son, I'm fine. We're the People. [*Normal voice*] You see.

LORETTA. Hank!

HANK. What, Ma? [*Falsetto*] Loretta looks

141

dirty, son. Tell her to take a shower. [*Normal*] You need a shower, Loretta.

LORETTA. Hank, you need help. Psychiatric help.

HANK. You want to say hello to Ma, Loretta? Ma, Loretta wants to see you. [*Falsetto*] Let me just put on my lip rouge, son. Hello, Loretta. Nice to see you.

[LORETTA *screams, runs to another seat.* HANK *has raised his knife to kill* LORETTA *but she hasn't seen him. Enter* EVE *and the* THEATER MANAGER. HANK *puts his knife away.*]

EVE. [*Pointing at* BETTE.] There she is.

MANAGER. [*To* BETTE] I'm sorry, miss. We'll have to ask you to leave now.

BETTE. What? Is the picture over?

MANAGER. Yes, it's over.

BETTE. [*Looking at screen.*] What are all those people doing up there?

MANAGER. They're worshiping molten images. Come on.

BETTE. [*Licks her lips lasciviously.*] Do you think I'm Elizabeth Taylor in *Raintree*

County? I could be Joanne Woodward in *Three Faces of Eve*. Hello, I'm Eve White. Hi there, I'm Eve Black. Hi ... [*Exits with* MANAGER.]

HANK. Loretta, Ma wants you to come back and sit with us. [*Falsetto*] Come on back, Loretta honey. I won't bite you.

LORETTA. Oh, God.

HANK. [*Falsetto*] Don't be sad, son. You'll see Loretta again. [*Normal*] I know, Ma.

EVE. Sssssssshhhh.

HANK. [*Falsetto*] Hello, Eve. Nice to see you today.

EVE. Nice to see you, Mrs. Joad. Now if you and your son will both do me the favor of being quiet, I will consider my life fulfilled. Alright?

HANK. [*Falsetto*] Alright. [*Regular*] Alright.

CLARA. [*Depressed*] Why do they call it the *Red* Sea?

MICKEY. Clara, our marriage just hasn't worked out.

CLARA. It's just postwar adjustment problems.

MICKEY. Clara, we can't keep saying everything is postwar adjustment problems.

CLARA. Well then, it's tension about the bomb. Sputnik, Castro, Khrushchev not liking *Can Can*. It's more than I can stand.

EVE. Ssssssssssssh.

MICKEY. Clara, you're just not a good wife. You commit adultery, you're an alcoholic, you neglect the children. . . .

CLARA. I'm sorry, I just don't like the children.

MICKEY. Maybe if I'd had hands it would have been different. Good-bye, Clara. [*Exits;* CLARA *cries.*]

EVE. [*Mad*] Why are you crying? The movie is not sad.
[CLARA *runs out.*]

HANK. [*Muttering in falsetto*] We're the People. Ya can't keep us down, ya can't lick us. . . .

EVE. BE QUIET!

HANK. [*Looks at her with hatred; falsetto*] Go

get her, son. [HANK *takes out knife, stabs her repeatedly.*]

[STUART *sees the stabbing, looks away, keeps his eyes riveted on the screen.* LORETTA, *who is seated on one side of* STUART, *stares ahead, seemingly not noticing the killing.*]

[JIMMY *enters from back of movie theater in a temper, looking for* LORETTA. *On his entrance,* HANK *stops stabbing and sits the dead* EVE *up in her seat.*]

[*Enter* JIMMY *from back of movie theater.*]

JIMMY. Loretta. I want you to come home.

LORETTA. I'm watching the movie, Jimmy.

JIMMY. The children miss you, Loretta. They miss their mother.

LORETTA. Screw the children.

JIMMY. Watch your mouth, Loretta.

LORETTA. Screw you!
[JIMMY *sits on other side of* STUART. STUART *is seated between* LORETTA *and* JIMMY.]

JIMMY. You're gonna get it when we get home.

LORETTA. Screw you, cluck!
[*Enter* BETTE *from back of auditorium, in a*

wheelchair. The THEATER MANAGER *follows behind, upset.*]

MANAGER. Miss, miss.
[BETTE *fires a gun, killing him.* LORETTA *and*
JIMMY *don't notice,* STUART *thinks he's in a nut-
house.* BETTE *settles herself comfortably in her
wheelchair in the front-row aisle.*]

BETTE. What a dump!
[BETTE *does the Bette Davis circular-hand
gesture, maniacally, and it turns into the
Dr. Strangelove-strangling-himself gesture. She
should probably wear a black leather glove on
her strangling hand. When she stops strangling
herself, she should push a button on a small de-
vice in her hand.*]

LORETTA. Hey, what's that from?

JIMMY. What's what from?

LORETTA. She just did it for you. What a
dump!

JIMMY. I don't know what it's from.

LORETTA. It's from some goddamn Bette Davis
movie. [*To* STUART] Hey, you, what's it from?

STUART. Excuse me?

146

LORETTA. Yeah, you. What's it from? What a dump!

STUART. [*Uncomfortable*] I don't know. Is it from *Lilies of the Field*?

LORETTA. No, cluck, it's not from *Lilies of the Field*.

STUART. [*Standing, to leave.*] Excuse me.

JIMMY. Sit down.

STUART. *Excuse* me.

JIMMY. Stop him, Bette.
[BETTE *shoots gun in his direction, doesn't hit him.* STUART *sits down, further alarmed.*]

LORETTA. [*To* STUART] We have the most lovely daughter.

JIMMY. Yeah, a real knockout.

LORETTA. Would you like to come to dinner and marry her? We don't care you're Negro, do we, Jimmy?

JIMMY. Hell, no, we're very liberal.

LORETTA. Goddamn right.

HANK. [*Who's moved to a seat behind* LORETTA; *in falsetto*] Hello, Loretta.

LORETTA. Not now, Hank. [*To* STUART] Or if not our daughter Deirdre, how about our son Bob?

JIMMY. Sure, come to dinner and marry Bob.

LORETTA. If Bob would want it, we would want it.

STUART. What's the matter with you two?

LORETTA. Do you have children?

STUART. No.

LORETTA. We have twelve children. There's Robert and Deirdre and Ernestine and Joel and Barbara and Maxine and William and Michael and David and Lily and Martha and Susie.

JIMMY. You know what they say. . . .

JIMMY and LORETTA. IT'S CHEAPER BY THE DOZEN! [*Laugh hilariously.*]

BETTE. You have children? Take that and that and that. . . . [*Pushes button.*]

JIMMY. Whatcha got there, Bette?

BETTE. This is the button. I got access to the button. I'm a member of the Joint Chiefs of Staff now. We bomb things.

LORETTA. Hello, Bette. Have you met our son-in-law?

BETTE. Where your parents from, black boy?

STUART. Chicago.

BETTE. Not anymore. [*Pushes button.*]

HANK. There's a fly on my nose, Ma. [*Falsetto*] Just leave it be, son, it'll go away.

JIMMY. You know some people may not want you to marry our daughter, black boy, but you know what I say to those people?

LORETTA. You tell 'im, Jimmy.

JIMMY. They can eat shit!

LORETTA. That's tellin' 'em, baby!

JIMMY. Eat shit, eat shit, eat shit.

LORETTA. [*Suddenly exhausted; to* STUART] You know sometimes I wish the thirties had never ended. It was so much clearer when we were gangsters or screwballs, but now ... [*Teary*] I don't know what we're doing. ...

JIMMY. Eat shit, Loretta!

LORETTA. [*Vicious*] Screw you, Jimmy!

STUART. Please! I don't come to the movies for this kind of thing!

JIMMY. No? Well, what do you come for, then, huh? You come for a skin flick? Well, we can fix that. Why don't you hump my wife? Hey, Loretta, he wants you to spread for him.

LORETTA. Oh, Jimmy, you're sick, you're really sick.

JIMMY. Is that the game we should play first?

LORETTA. Well, you sure as hell can't play it. [*To* STUART] You wanna know why?

JIMMY. Don't tell him, Loretta.

HANK. The fly's still there, Ma.

LORETTA. You wanna know why?

JIMMY. Cut it, Loretta.

LORETTA. Because I am more of a man than my husband is. Tell them about your souvenir from the war, Jimmy.

JIMMY. You went too far, Loretta.

LORETTA. Tell them about your dead badge of courage. Tell them our marriage is nothing but a limp noodle.

JIMMY. I'm going to kill the children, Loretta.

HANK. Got it. [*Kills fly on his nose, eats it.*]

JIMMY. I'm going to kill them.

LORETTA. I don't care, go ahead.

JIMMY. All right, I've just killed Robert.

LORETTA. Go ahead! I've killed Ernestine.

JIMMY. I've killed Joel and Maxine!

LORETTA. I've killed William!

JIMMY. I've killed David!

BETTE. [*Pushing button.*] I got Thailand!

LORETTA. Barbara's dead!

JIMMY. Michael's dead!

151

LORETTA. Susie's dead!

BETTE. I got Norway!

JIMMY. Deirdre's dead! Deirdre's dead, git outa here, boy.

STUART. I don't come to the movies for this sort of thing!

BETTE. [*In a Mercedes McCambridge voice*] I'm the devil, fuck me, fuck me!

LORETTA. [*Hysterical*] I want a proper life. I want every transgression to be punished I want no conversation to have salacious content I want never to discuss themes of incest or white slavery or . . .

HANK. [*Falsetto*] Take a shower, Loretta!
[HANK *stabs* LORETTA *repeatedly.*]

JIMMY. [*Suddenly riveted to screen; quiets everyone.*] Sssssssh. Look, an earthquake.
[*Everyone looks at screen.* SOUND *of earthquake. The earthquake spreads from the screen to the theater. Everyone in theater shakes wildly. The* BLESSED MOTHER *is unaffected and sits calmly in her movie seat. There are various explosions, and at the peak of the destruction the projection booth explodes, spewing unreeling film all over the stage. Also, large chunks of the letters from*

the THE END *sign fall down from the sky. After
the earthquake is over, the* BLESSED MOTHER *applauds it calmly, and exits. Everyone is still,
seemingly dead. Then* JIMMY, BETTE, HANK, *and*
LORETTA *begin to stir.*]

JIMMY. Well, I feel better after that. You know,
sometimes you have to knock everything down
in order to get a perspective on things.

LORETTA. Did The End sign fall to pieces?

JIMMY. [*Not quite paying attention to her*]
Yeah, I guess so. [*Enthusiastically planning
the future*] We'll have to start all over again—
building towns, railroads, inventing the telephone, the airplane, the electric light.

LORETTA. I really don't want to start over
again, Jimmy. I want the The End sign to
come down, and then I can stay frozen behind
it forever and then nothing else will happen
to me.

JIMMY. [*Sympathetically*] Ya can't have that,
kid. [*Back to his plans*] So—we'll invent the
telephone, and we'll raise cattle, and we'll
plant wheat and corn. And we'll have to procreate. I can't, of course, as Loretta was saying before the earthquake. But Hank, here, is
a man, and we have two women.

[*During the above,* LORETTA *picks up broken*

pieces of the The End sign, and tries to match them and put them back together. She keeps looking up occasionally too.]

BETTE. I want to sing like Jeanette MacDonald after the earthquake at the end of *San Francisco*.

JIMMY. We don't have time for that.

BETTE. Well, I want to.

JIMMY. Wait until I've finished. [*Envisioning the future*] So the three of you will have children and I'll oversee everything. And what a race we can engender.

HANK. [*Falsetto*] We're the People. [*Not falsetto*] Where's Ma?

JIMMY. That's right, Hank. And we'll have great leaders. Like Henry Fonda in *Young Mr. Lincoln*.

BETTE. [*Singing*] San Francisco, open your . . .

JIMMY. Oh alright, Bette.
[BETTE *sings "San Francisco," making up what she can't remember.*]

HANK. [*Falsetto*] Hank, boy, we gotta raise

some money. [*Regular*] I know, Ma, but how? Maybe if I auction some things.

JIMMY. That's right Hank. And we'll share our money like Gary Cooper in *Mr. Deeds Goes to Town*.

[*At this point many of the characters from earlier in the play begin to crawl in, out of the earthquake rubble:* MICKEY, CLARA, VIOLA, ALLISON, MICHAEL, *the* POLICEMAN *from the silent section,* DAVID, ERIC. *The* BLESSED MOTHER *leads in* JESUS, *also last seen in the silent section.*]

HANK. This is the iron Loretta used in *A Man's Castle*. Do I hear three hundred dollars?

JIMMY. Our race will have pioneer spirit like Edna May Oliver in *Drums Along the Mohawk*.

HANK. Do I hear fifty dollars? Do I hear fifty cents? [*Falsetto*] Fifty cents! [*Regular*] Sold to Ma Joad for fifty cents!

JIMMY.	CHORUS.
They'll have spiritual values like Spencer Tracy in *Boys Town*.	[*Singing*] spiritual values...

They'll be idealistic like James Stewart in *Mr. Smith Goes to Washington.*

Idealistic...

They'll be for racial tolerance like Gregory Peck in *To Kill a Mockingbird.*

Racial tolerance...

They'll suffer with patience like Luise Rainer in *The Good Earth*—the locusts ...

Suffer with patience...

They'll search for wisdom like Tyrone Power in *The Razor's Edge.* They'll take disappointment with dignity like Mickey Rooney in *Love Finds Andy Hardy.* They'll discover radium like Greer Garson in ... uh, *Madame Curie.* They'll invent penicillin like Paul Muni in, in ... *The Story of Louis Pasteur* ...

We'll search for wisdom
Like Tyrone Power,
Take disappointment
Like Mickey Rooney,
Discover radium
Like Greer Garson,
We'll invent penicillin
Like Paul Muni,

... in *Lost Horizon*,

We'll search for wisdom
Like Ronald Colman,

... in, uh, *Stagecoach*,

Have pioneer spirit
Like John Wayne,

... in *Watch on the Rhine*,

We'll be tough-minded
Like Lucille Watson,

... in, uh, uh, *Four Daughters* ...

We'll live by moral values
Like Priscilla Lane,

HANK.
[*Ripping off* CLARA's *dress.*] This is Clara's dress. Do I hear sixty cents?

We'll start again,
We'll start anew,
We'll search for wisdom,
For what is true,
We'll relive our past and keep the best,
And edit out the rest. ...

JIMMY.
Ssssh. Our children will be like Jackie Cooper in *Skippy;* Patty McCormack in *The Bad Seed*—uh, no, no—Dicky Moore, little Dicky Moore in *Blonde Venus* ...

Glory, glory, glory
  Lionel Barrymore,
Glory, glory, glory
  Dorothy Lamour,
Glory, glory, glory
  little Dicky Moore,
And we shall rise once more. ...

157

BLESSED MOTHER.
Our Father, who art in heaven,
give us this Doris Day Your Grace and Nancy Kelly;

And Robert Donat into temptation,
But deliver us Gene Tierney,
As it was in the beginning,
Is now, and ever shall be,
Forever and ever, Zasu Pitts,
Amen.

LORETTA.
[Holding piece of letter E.]
Here's part of the E, but where's the D?

O God, please grant a simple plea,

HANK.
[Takes off his pants.]
These are my pants. Do I hear thirty cents?

LORETTA.
Why can't The End sign finally rescue me?

[LORETTA goes up to the BLESSED MOTHER and JESUS.]

LORETTA. Will someone get me out of this?

JESUS. Right, dear.
[JESUS and the BLESSED MOTHER make a sign, and the THE END sign, now charred and missing some of its letters, descends from above. As the CHORUS sings, LORETTA is helped by the BLESSED MOTHER to attach herself to the THE END sign; and as the music peaks, LORETTA begins to ascend, happily, with the sign.]

CHORUS.
We'll search for wis-
dom
Like Leslie Howard,
Take disappointment
Like James Dean,
We'll be tough-minded
Like Wallace Beery,
We'll live by moral
values
Like Butterfly Mc-
Queen,
We'll search for wis-
dom
Like Marjorie Main,
Take disappointment
Like Joan Fontaine,
What Time's put asun-
der we shall mend,
Triumphant to The—

[LORETTA *starts to as-
cend, as the* BLESSED
MOTHER *waves her
up.*]
[EVE, *weak from her
stab wounds, begins
crawling through the
mess, looking desper-
ately up at the screen.*]

EVE. SHUT UP!
[*Everything stops, including LORETTA and the
sign.*]
I want . . . to see . . . the next feature!
[*All look at* EVE *for a second, sit down in the
nearest seat, and then look out at the screen.
The* BLESSED MOTHER *and* JESUS *also stare out,
having lost interest in the ascension.* LORETTA *is
now stuck between below and whatever on the
unmoving* THE END *sign; she motions furiously*

for it to go up, and tries to get the attention of the BLESSED MOTHER and JESUS, but to no avail.

Finally LORETTA gives up and bitterly looks out at the screen also. The projector light flips on; we hear the sound of the film going through the projector, and lights dim.]